WITHDRAWN
WRIGHT STATE UNIVERSITY LIBRARIES

COLS WRIGHT STATE UNIVERSITY
UNIVERSITY LIBRARY

0 00 13 0108866 0

DATE DUE

SEP 2 3 1993			

D1116166

HIGHSMITI

Mary Stewart

Twayne's English Authors Series

Kinley E. Roby, Editor

Northeastern University

TEAS 474

Mary Stewart
Photograph courtesy of Hodder & Stoughton Limited

Mary Stewart

By Lenemaja Friedman
Columbus College

Twayne Publishers
A Division of G. K. Hall & Co. • *Boston*

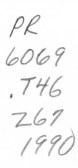

PR
6069
.T46
Z67
1990

Mary Stewart
Lenemaja Friedman

Copyright 1990 by G. K. Hall & Co.
All rights reserved.
Published by Twayne Publishers
A Division of G. K. Hall & Co.
70 Lincoln Street
Boston, Massachusetts 02111

Copyediting supervised by Barbara Sutton
Book production by Janet Z. Reynolds
Book design by Barbara Anderson

Typeset in 11 pt. Garamond
by Compset, Inc., Beverly, Massachusetts

Printed on permanent/durable acid-free paper
and bound in the United States of America

First published 1990.
10 9 8 7 6 5 4 3 2 1

Library of Congress Cataloging-in-Publication Data

Friedman, Lenemaja.
    Mary Stewart / by Lenemaja Friedman.
        p.   cm.—(Twayne's English authors series ; TEAS 474)
    Includes bibliographical references.
    ISBN 0-8057-6985-4 (alk. paper)
    1.   Stewart, Mary, 1916– —Criticism and interpretation.
    2.   Arthurian romances—Adaptations—History and criticism.
    I.   Title.   II.   Series.
    PR6069.T46Z67   1990
    823'.914—dc20   89-39763
                                                                        CIP

*For my
sister-in-law and brother—
Roselynn and Alex von Heister*

Contents

About the Author

Lenemaja von Heister Friedman was born in Germany and moved with her family to Newark, New Jersey, in 1927. Her growing-up years were spent in the Catskill Mountains of New York State. She attended Syracuse University and then transferred to the University of Washington (Seattle), where she received her bachelor's degree. She spent the next four years as a production manager in an advertising agency in Manhattan and later worked as a tax collector, a librarian, and a high school English teacher in the Catskills. She attended Cornell University briefly and the State University of New York at Albany for her master's degree; she received her Ph.D. from Florida State University in 1969. At present Friedman is chair of the Department of Language and Literature at Columbus College, Columbus, Georgia. She is the author of numerous short stories and articles, and her books include *Shirley Jackson* (1975) and *Enid Bagnold* (1986).

Preface

Mary Stewart says of herself that she is a born storyteller. From the age of five she knew that she wanted to be a writer or a painter, but not until many years later—after her university days, her first teaching experiences, and several years of marriage—did she attempt to write her first adult novel. This was *Madam, Will You Talk?* (1955); she was then "off and running," so to speak, for that novel and every novel thereafter became best-sellers. Stewart started out at the top and has remained there. She writes to give pleasure, she says, but she is a professional author serious about her gift and her craft.

During the early half of her career, Stewart wrote successful tales of mystery and suspense. Since 1970 she has concentrated on the equally successful Arthurian novel series: *The Crystal Cave, The Hollow Hills, The Last Enchantment* (the novels about Merlin), and *The Wicked Day* (the novel about Mordred and Arthur).

As a writer, she is noted for her dynamic, often exotic settings, which play a vital part in the storytelling. She is likewise skillful at creating plot and suspense. Her women protagonists are strong, heroic people, protective of those weaker or younger than they. The same is true of many of the women characters in the Arthurian novels.

The major characters in the Arthurian works are believable people, not simply mythic figures, and Stewart's treatment of the Celtic world of late fifth- and early sixth-century Britain is realistic and memorable, the product of much research and a creative imagination.

Mary Stewart's works continue to be in demand. Even those written in the 1950s are difficult to find in used-book stores, for they are purchased again as soon as they appear. Her novels in public libraries also remain in constant circulation, and each novel has gone through many printings.

This book is the first full-length treatment of Mary Stewart's work. I approach the material chronologically, discussing first the novels of suspense and then the Arthurian works. I hope to show that Mary Stewart, in addition to being an expert at suspense, is a skilled prose stylist and a master teller of tales.

Lenemaja Friedman

Columbus College

ix

Acknowledgments

I wish to thank Columbus College for the Faculty Development Grant, making possible the Edinburgh trip in June 1987; Callie McGinnis and Merne Posey of the Columbus College library for their help with interlibrary loans and the obtaining of materials; the staff of the University of Edinburgh library and all those who helped to make my Scotland visit a pleasant one: my family and friends for their patience during the busy months of writing; my colleague David Johnson for his help with proofreading; and to my friend Libby Eno for typing the manuscript.

I am grateful to Hodder & Stoughton and William Morrow & Company, Inc., for permission to reprint excerpts from the following Mary Stewart novels:

Madam, Will You Talk? by Mary Stewart, © 1956. Reprinted by permission of Hodder & Stoughton and William Morrow & Company, Inc.

Wildfire at Midnight by Mary Stewart, © 1961. Reprinted by permission of Hoddard & Stoughton and William Morrow & Company, Inc.

Nine Coaches Waiting by Mary Stewart, © 1959. Reprinted by permission of Hoddard & Stoughton and William Morrow & Company, Inc.

My Brother Michael by Mary Stewart, © 1960. Reprinted by permission of Hoddard & Stoughton and William Morrow & Company, Inc.

The Ivy Tree by Mary Stewart, © 1962. Reprinted by permission of Hoddard & Stoughton and William Morrow & Company, Inc.

The Moon Spinners by Mary Stewart, © 1963. Reprinted by permission of Hoddard & Stoughton and William Morrow & Company, Inc.

The Gabriel Hounds by Mary Stewart, © 1967. Reprinted by permission of Hoddard & Stoughton and William Morrow & Company, Inc.

Touch Not the Cat by Mary Stewart, © 1976. Reprinted by permission of Hoddard & Stoughton and William Morrow & Company, Inc.

The Crystal Cave by Mary Stewart, © 1970. Reprinted by permission of Hoddard & Stoughton and William Morrow & Company, Inc.

The Hollow Hills by Mary Stewart, © 1973. Reprinted by permission of Hoddard & Stoughton and William Morrow & Company, Inc.

The Last Enchantment by Mary Stewart, © 1979. Reprinted by permission of Hoddard & Stoughton and William Morrow & Company, Inc.

The Wicked Day by Mary Stewart, © 1983. Reprinted by permission of Hoddard & Stoughton and William Morrow & Company, Inc.

Chronology

1916   Mary Stewart born 17 September in Sunderland, County Durham, England.

1921   Attends village school in Trimdon where father is vicar. Writes first stories. Is determined to be a writer and/or painter. (First publication is a poem called "Teeth.")

1923   Moves to Shotton Colliery, mining village; attends village school briefly.

1924   Attends boarding school, a very unhappy experience.

1926   Leaves school because of near breakdown; receives scholarship to Eden Hall, Cumberland, the buildings and surroundings of which later serve as background for *The Ivy Tree*.

1929   Makes school history by passing all six grades of the Royal Drawing Society examinations by age thirteen. Drawings are exhibited in Junior Exhibitions at Burlington House.

1930   School goes bankrupt. At fourteen, Stewart emerges with a creditable School Certificate with Distinction in English, French, and art.

1935   Attends Durham University to study English.

1938   Receives First Class Honours B.A. Becomes president of the Women's Union.

1939   Is awarded First Class Teaching Diploma, majoring in English with a minor in art. Receives position teaching arithmetic, sewing, and music in elementary boarding school.

1940   Receives position as Senior English Mistress at girls' (secondary) boarding school in West Midlands.

1941   Receives M.A. from Durham University. Writes much poetry during this time. Receives an invitation to return to Durham University as a lecturer in the English department; also teaches the Sixth Form at Durham School (the boys' public school) part-time. Besides lecturing and writing, works at night for the Royal Observer Corps.

1945   Attends VE Day celebration dance; meets geology lecturer
        Frederick Henry Stewart, whom she marries in September
        1945. Continues teaching and living in Durham.

1948   Begins writing her first story for children, *The Enchanted
        Journey.*

1949   Continues teaching part-time and working with the University
        Dramatic Society.

1951   Begins work on *Murder for Charity,* renamed *Madam, Will You
        Talk?*

1953   Receives first contract, on Christmas Eve, from Hodder and
        Stoughton.

1955   *Madam, Will You Talk?* is published. Stewart travels to Greece,
        the first of many trips. Has begun writing *Thunder on the Right*
        but puts it aside.

1956   *Wildfire at Midnight* is published. Stewart begins writing *Nine
        Coaches Waiting.* Moves in autumn to Edinburgh, where Fred-
        erick Stewart is appointed Regius Professor in Geology at Edin-
        burgh University.

1957   *Thunder on the Right* is published.

1958   *Nine Coaches Waiting* is published, story excerpt appears in the
        Ladies' Home Journal. Four short radio plays are produced on
        the British Broadcasting Corporation network (*Lift from a
        Stranger, Call Me at Ten-thirty, The Crime of Mr. Merry,* and *The
        Lord of Langdale*).

1960   *My Brother Michael,* written as a result of Stewart's visit to
        Greece, is published.

1961   *The Ivy Tree* is published. Receives the Crime Writers Associa-
        tion Silver Dagger; story excerpt appears in the *Ladies' Home
        Journal.*

1962   *The Moon-Spinners* is published. In spring Stewart visits Corfu,
        its setting serving to suggest the theme of *This Rough Magic.*
        Excerpt of *The Moon-Spinners* appears in the *Ladies' Home
        Journal.*

1963   Movie version of *The Moon-Spinners* is released.

1964   *This Rough Magic* (one of Stewart's favorite books) is published,
        becomes a Literary Guild selection, and is on the *New York
        Times* best-seller list for eight months.

1965 *Airs above the Ground* is published and for eight months is on the *New York Times* best-seller list.

1966 Story excerpt of *Airs above the Ground* appears in *Good Housekeeping.*

1967 *The Gabriel Hounds* is published, becoming a Doubleday Book Club selection, a *Readers' Digest* Condensed Book Club selection, and a Literary Guild alternate selection.

1968 *The Wind off the Small Isles* is published (though not in America); story excerpt appears in *Good Housekeeping.* Stewart is elected Fellow of the Royal Society of Arts.

1970 *The Crystal Cave* (the original idea for which occurred ten years earlier), is published, becomes a selection of the Literary Guild, and for ten months is on the *New York Times* best-seller list; story excerpt appears in the *Ladies' Home Journal.*

1971 *The Crystal Cave* receives the Frederick Niven Award and is a selection of the Doubleday Bargain Book Club. *The Little Broomstick* (juvenile fiction) is published.

1973 *The Hollow Hills* is published and becomes a selection of the Literary Guild.

1974 *The Hollow Hills* becomes a selection of the Doubleday Bargain Book Club. *Ludo and the Star Horse* (juvenile fiction) is published. Frederick Stewart is knighted for his service to science.

1975 *Ludo and the Star Horse* receives the Scottish Arts Council Award.

1976 *Touch Not the Cat* is published; story excerpt is serialized in *Good Housekeeping* in July and August.

1979 *The Last Enchantment* is published and for seven months is on the *New York Times* best-seller list.

1980 *A Walk in Wolf Wood* (juvenile fiction) is published.

1983 *The Wicked Day* is published and for fifteen weeks is on the *New York Times* best-seller list.

1988 *Thornyhold* is published in England and America.

Chapter One

About Mary Stewart

The Family

Mary Florence Elinor Rainbow—Mary Stewart—was born on 17 September 1916 in Sunderland, County Durham, England. Her father, Frederick Albert Rainbow, was an Anglican clergyman then serving as curate of St. Thomas's Church in Sunderland. His ancestors were Englishmen from Buckinghamshire. Mary Stewart's mother, Mary Edith Matthews, came from a New Zealand family of pioneers who settled on the North Island in the middle of the nineteenth century; her ancestors had been of mixed stock, including Polish, Danish, Irish, Welsh, and German. One member of her family had been on the voyage of *The Beagle* with Charles Darwin. His brother, Mary Stewart's great-grandfather, founded Kaitaia, on the northern tip of the North Island, New Zealand. Her maternal grandfather, Richard Blencoe Matthews, had been a botanist and plant hunter. It is little wonder, then, that Mary Stewart developed a love for natural history.

Her father also shared the spirit of adventure, for at the age of nineteen he, with a group from England, had sailed round Cape Horn and on to New Zealand, intent on seeking his fortune, and there he met his future wife, Mary Stewart's mother. By the time of Mary Stewart's birth, however, he had moved back to England with his wife and had begun his career in the church.

The Early Days

When Mary Stewart was still a baby, the family moved to the small agricultural village of Trimdon, also in Durham County, where her father served as vicar for seven years. Mary attended the local village school when she was five, although at this stage of her life she was already able to read and write. Later, she spent hours in the attic of the vicarage writing and illustrating stories in an old exercise book. She remembers three toys—a little rubber horse, a tin elephant, and a rubber cat—that became the characters of her first fairy tales, animal stories, and poems. In the beginning she would draw the stories and then write a narrative to accompany the pictures; writing came easily, and she soon decided she would become an artist, a writer, or both. One of her poems, called "Teeth," was published in the parish magazine. Another long narrative poem, one she was often required to recite in public, was, she recalls, about a horse. The poem may have been forgotten, but her love of horses was lifelong.

The home environment was one of warmth and affection. The children now included, besides Mary, a brother and a sister, yet Mary seems to have enjoyed spending time alone. For a time she and her brother read a chapter of the Bible aloud to their mother every evening. Slipshod speech or slang, she recalls, was not allowed in their household; nevertheless, they received much encouragement from their parents.

When Mary was seven the family moved to Shotton Colliery, a mining town in the same county. The vicarage here was "huge, isolated and bitterly cold."[1] Mary's room was in the attic, two stories up, but the temperature and elevation apparently had no serious effects on her spirits or creativity. What did seriously affect her, however, was the atmosphere of the boarding school to which she was sent the following year. She spent two unhappy years at that school, the name of which she prefers not to reveal. After a near breakdown, she left and soon thereafter applied for and won a scholarship to Eden Hall in Cumberland. Here began a peaceful sojourn in this beautiful hall, with its parklike surroundings, part of which she re-created for her novel *The Ivy Tree*. Training in the social graces was of primary importance here, with lesser emphasis on regular studies. Among the required skills, she says, were making a proper court curtsy, filling out a dance program, "laying a ghost," and playing ice hockey. On her own she managed also to learn to groom horses, although officially trips to the stables were forbidden for those students not receiving regular riding lessons. She was able also to take advantage of the adjoining woods and parks, spending time watching and drawing birds and other small animals. In her school subjects she received excellent training in English and French and good instruction in art but poor training in science, mathematics, and geography. For her particular talents, however, the schooling reinforced the skills most needed in her career as a writer.

She recalls that she made school history by passing "all six grades of the Royal Drawing Society examinations by the age of thirteen"[2] and that drawings of hers had been entered in an exhibition at Burlington

House. After four years here she finished at fourteen with a creditable School Certificate with Distinction in English, French, and art. The school, in the meantime, had gone bankrupt. She then found a place (a bursary) at Skellfield School in Yorkshire, which she describes as a good, well-run school. She was happy there, becoming involved in sports and demonstrating leadership qualities by being chosen Head of House and House Cricket and Tennis Captain.

University and the Beginning of a Career

In 1935 Mary Stewart went to Durham University to study English and in 1938 received a First Class Honours B.A. Again becoming involved in college life and leadership activities, she was elected president of the Women's Union; she was at one time also president of the Literary Society and active in college theatricals. (In addition, she was a swimmer for the university—a good one, in the process even breaking a swimming-speed record.) In 1939 she received a First Class Teaching Diploma in English with a First Class distinction as well in her secondary field, art. She realized she had a living to earn, and that included plans to become a teacher.

She was writing a great deal of poetry now and in fantasy saw herself not as a writer or a great painter but as a professor of poetry at Oxford. Acquiring a job, however, was no easy matter. World War II had begun, and there were almost no school openings. Then she received a position at an elementary school in Middlesbrough, but instead of being assigned the subjects for which she had been trained, she was given arithmetic, sewing, and music. It was a difficult year, the winter was very cold, and having the flu made it worse. Conditions were aggravated by the fear of air raids and for a time the necessity to sleep underground in a homemade dugout; then, until the school could build air-raid shelters, classes were taught at various houses in the neighborhood. The small groups themselves were informal and enjoyable, with parents cooperating as well as possible; but each class had to be taught several times.

Throughout the year Mary continued to apply for secondary-level teaching positions. Then in September 1940 she was offered a position in the West Midlands as Senior English Mistress in a girls' boarding school. Here she was asked, in addition to other duties, to teach all the Latin in the school up to university level, although she herself had taken only two years of Latin, and to teach all the middle and senior

English classes, as well as supervising breaks, being in charge of games or walks in the afternoon, and being librarian. The year passed, and then fortunately, Durham University invited her to teach part-time in the English department, which had lost personnel to the armed forces. Mary was delighted, especially since her assignment involved second-year honors students. The salary was meager, however; she therefore took a second job, teaching the Sixth Form at Durham School, the boys' public school. By this time, Mary Stewart's sister had married a farmer in the nearby area and, as Mary admits, "I didn't starve, but I lived on the edge of hardship, and would have done badly without my sister's help."³ Otherwise, for Mary it was a "wonderful" experience. She loved her students. And besides teaching, she worked at night for the Royal Observer Corps, whose members reported aircraft movements and gave locations of crashed planes or those in distress. In 1941 she had continued her studies and received an M.A. in English from the Durham University.

New Directions

By 1945 and war's end, Mary's job at the university was over and she was searching for a new position. At the VE Day celebration given by the students, she met Frederick Henry Stewart, her future husband. It was a costume party, and as she says: "He was not hard to spot; he was the chap wearing a girl's gym tunic and a red ribbon in his hair. He looked quite dreadful, but he had a lovely voice."⁴ She had come as the Merry Widow. She quickly decided that Frederick was the man she wanted to marry, and he made the same decision. She canceled two pending job interviews, and they were married three months later, in September 1945.

After their marriage, the couple continued to live in Durham for eleven years. Mary kept up with her teaching, lecturing part-time at St. Hild's College and then again at Durham University. When the couple bought a house, Mary became involved with gardening, which she considers the best and most satisfying of all hobbies. In 1947 she had an ectopic pregnancy that resulted, unfortunately, in a serious illness involving three operations, after which she was told she would remain childless. A year later she resumed her teaching and was working with the University Dramatic Society. In addition, she began to write her first children's tale, *The Enchanted Journey,* inspired by a Walter de la Mare story, *Henry Brocken.* For Mary, storytelling had always come naturally, and now she began on a new project, writing in earnest. This was to be her first novel, originally titled *Murder for Charity* and then retitled *Madam, Will You Talk?* Its writing took two years, but even then she was not thinking seriously of publication until her husband urged her to send the manuscript to a publisher. While the novel was under consideration she began writing another book. On Christmas Eve 1953, Hodder and Stoughton sent her a contract for *Madam, Will You Talk?* Mary put aside the present book, *Thunder on the Right*, for further reworking and then wrote *Wildfire at Midnight*.

In 1956 the Stewarts moved to Edinburgh, where Frederick had been appointed Regius Professor in Geology at Edinburgh University. By this time Mary had finished the novel *Thunder on the Right* and was halfway through *Nine Coaches Waiting*. She had decided now to spend all her time writing. She had much encouragement, for each novel had become a best-seller. She had also begun traveling; in 1955 she had flown to Greece, a country she later visited many times. That setting and others in France, Lebanon, and Austria became the backgrounds for her first novels. The Scottish background for *Wildfire at Midnight* (the Isle of Skye) was territory she and her husband had traveled together; as she says, they "covered every inch of Scotland."[5]

Over the years, more best-sellers emerged: *My Brother Michael* in 1960, *The Ivy Tree* in 1961, *The Moon-Spinners* in 1962 (which was made into a motion picture the following year), *This Rough Magic* in 1964, *Airs above the Ground* in 1965, *The Gabriel Hounds* in 1967, *The Wind off the Small Isles* (a novella) in 1968, *The Crystal Cave* (the first of the Arthurian novels) in 1970, *The Hollow Hills* in 1973, *Touch Not the Cat* in 1976, *The Last Enchantment* in 1979, and the last of the Arthurian novels, *The Wicked Day*, in 1983. Mary Stewart's novels have been translated into sixteen languages, including Hebrew, Icelandic, and Slovak. In addition to the novels, she has written four radio plays and three children's books. In 1968 she was elected a Fellow of the Royal Society of Arts, one of many honors she has received.

Additional Interests

Next to gardening, Mary Stewart's main hobby has been the study of natural history, or just being involved in the out-of-doors observing the wildlife and appreciating the plants and flowers. When she and her brother and sister were children, they were taught to identify various plants, and she later learned to identify trees and rocks. Stewart

also loves animals and enjoys watching wild animals in their own surroundings, a skill acquired through much practice. It is not surprising,
then, that her characters feel at home in the out-of-doors and that the
major chases in her suspense novels take place in the spaciousness of
the countryside.

Another great interest has been delving into the mysteries of ancient
Greece and Rome. Stewart grew up close to the Roman ruins in northern England, and the lure of the ancient Roman and Greek civilizations
prompted her to begin travels to that part of the world. In addition,
she has an appreciation for myths and folktales of all kinds. The re-
newed interest in ancient British history and in the late fifth and early
sixth centuries suggested her first historical novel, *The Crystal Cave*;
the immediate inspiration had been the reading of Geoffrey of Monmouth's *The History of the Kings of Britain* and his account of Merlin as
a boy—that is, the dramatic situation in which Merlin must defend
himself against King Vortigern, who wishes to sacrifice him.

When Stewart wrote this first Arthurian story about Merlin's boyhood and growing up, she intended it to be the last, ending as it does
with the conception of King Arthur and the promise of his being given
into Merlin's care. Fortunately, however, her additional study in
Arthurian legend encouraged her to continue the tale of Merlin's life
in *The Hollow Hills*. Stewart's next novel was another suspense story,
Touch Not the Cat, followed by *The Last Enchantment*, and from there
the story of Mordred in *The Wicked Day*, all of these also deeply involving the life of Arthur. Considering content and subject matter, one
finds a vast difference therefore between the earlier suspense novels and
the Arthurian novels.

Among Stewart's continued interests are her love of painting—perhaps a major contributor to the effectiveness of her descriptive passages—and her love of theater. Her dramatic experiences have
undoubtedly proved helpful to her in creating character, plot, and suspense in the novels.

Classification of the Novels

Stewart's Arthurian novels are clearly historical fiction or historical
romance, if one chooses to call them that. Classifying the early works,
however, is difficult; for instance, Stewart is listed in *Twentieth Century
Romance and Gothic Writers* as well as in *Twentieth Century Crime and
Mystery Writers*. In the former, Kay Mussell, who has also written the

preface to the volume, says that it is unfair to label Stewart a genre writer and that the highly popular novels of romantic suspense were, for the sake of convenience, often labeled gothics. Mussell points out, however, that although there are similarities to the novels of Victoria Holt and Phyllis Whitney, "Stewart transcended their work and the formula romance of which these were the three most significant writers."[6] She has praise also for Stewart's prose style and for the "charm and good humor with which her heroines tell their tales"; in addition, she says that "even in her weaker books" Stewart is "a writer of uncommon originality and grace."[7]

With respect to the crime and mystery classification, there is murder (either past or present) in almost all the suspense novels, but aside from *Wildfire at Midnight,* they cannot be considered mystery or detective stories. Further, although elements of love are present, these novels cannot be classified as typical popular romances. Nor do most of them contain the telltale marks of the gothic story. They do contain an abundance of adventure and suspense, which is why, for purposes of discussion, we have called them simply suspense novels. Mary Stewart herself has resisted the narrow classification of her stories, preferring to think of them as thrillers or entertainments and herself in the larger sphere of entertainer and storyteller.

Mussell in *Twentieth Century Romance and Gothic Writers* deplored the scarcity of critical materials available in the newer fields of study. She says: "Only recently, under the influence of the emerging fields of popular culture and women's studies, have scholars begun to look systematically and seriously at gothic and romance writers and readers. Because the area of study is so new, it is hampered by a paucity of bibliographical and critical materials."[8]

Ideas about Writing

As to suspense, one of the writers Mary Stewart much admires is Graham Greene. She says: "Look at all the suspense elements he uses. There's no difference in kind, really, in quality between Greene's serious novels and his 'entertainments.' They are all superbly written, and if they serve different purposes, we can't say that one is less good than another."[9] The same principle might apply as well to her own earlier novels and the Arthurian tales. They involve different techniques and have supposedly different purposes, although the underlying intent is to entertain.

As to character, Stewart has definite ideas about her protagonists' standards of conduct: She wants them to be honorable and ethical. These same standards hold for her characterizations of Merlin and Mordred, although Mordred might be termed "borderline." Both are, however, intensely sympathetic and believable, given the circumstances in which they find themselves and the handicaps they must overcome. They are essentially honorable people, as are Stewart's King Arthur and Guinevere. Stewart says also that it is not enough for a novelist to record only "plain reality" and that the things writers would like to see have as much a place in fiction as the things they do see. She maintains that in an age that devalues the individual, "the novelist has all the more responsibility . . . to create a world where the individual is still seen to matter, and where right is still paramount."[10]

Writing Habits and Techniques

With the suspense novels, Stewart says that she "tried to take conventionally bizarre situations (the car chase, the closed-room murder, the wicked uncle tale) and send real people into them, normal everyday people with normal everyday reactions to violence and fear; people not 'heroic' in the conventional sense, but averagely intelligent men and women who could be shocked or outraged into defending, if necessary with great physical bravery, what they held to be right."[11]

With these novels Stewart began primarily with the setting, which immediately suggested the plot; in fact, in her stories setting is an important part of the plot. Setting, says Stewart, "dictates its own kind of plot; and . . . to allow it to permeate every corner of the story could do nothing but enrich the story."[12] She believes she is fortunate to have a good visual memory, finding herself including details she wasn't aware she remembered. In the historical novels, she maintains, the "dynamic use of setting is a weapon" no novelist can afford to ignore.[13] But description is not enough; the senses must be invoked. "By exploiting the simple sensation," she states, "the writer can transport his reader into the character's skin, transcending barriers of personality, even of sex."[14] Perhaps the best testimonial to this advice to writers is Stewart's creation of the characters of Merlin and Mordred. Whereas in the suspense novels the protagonists are women, in the Arthurian novels the leading characters are men who are every bit as convincing—in fact, more so, given the psychological realism and the historical verisimilitude needed.

Mary Stewart keeps daily writing hours, the number of which depends on the stage of development of the novel she is working on. For her, a four-hour period is considered a "short burst" of writing and is the goal at the beginning or the most difficult parts of a book, or it may be two thousand words a day. Toward the end of a book she is so caught up in the writing that she puts in extra hours, finding it difficult to set the manuscript aside.

Mornings are spent doing domestic chores or working with her secretary on correspondence or dictation. Her regular writing time is from 2:00 to 6:00 P.M. and then often in the evening after dinner. She does four drafts of each book. The preplanning is important, and when she begins with the writing she has on hand chapter synopses, family trees of her characters, maps of places involved, notes of all kinds, and the workings out of the major scenes.

The first rough-draft stage lasts approximately three or four months. When the real writing begins, she says, the work is slow and often difficult, as she may create only a paragraph a day. In later stages she rewrites each chapter and then cuts, shapes, and tightens the material, checks details, and examines characters for consistency.

Apparently she enjoys finding the quotations she uses as chapter headings for the suspense novels. These quoted lines, from many sources, serve various purposes depending on the contents of the particular chapter and are one of the trademarks of these stories. For instance, in *This Rough Magic,* set in Corfu, the island Shakespeare may have had in mind for *The Tempest,* all the chapter headings are quotations from *The Tempest,* aptly chosen to fit the material therein. Most of the quotations for *My Brother Michael,* which takes place in Greece, are from the plays of Euripides, Sophocles, and Aristophanes. The most diverse representations are those from *Airs above the Ground,* which takes place in Austria; here are more than fifteen different sources, ranging from seven Shakespearean plays to the extravagant humor of Mark Twain and Artemus Ward. Sometimes the quotations are intended to create suspense, sometimes to emphasize emotional content, and sometimes merely to suggest events to follow, but often the lines are playful, humorous, or ironic: one way Stewart reminds the reader that the story is, after all, a fabrication, an entertainment.

Writing continues to be a major focus of Stewart's life, and one can expect many more novels to come, for a true storyteller remains a storyteller for life, or at least for as long as mind, body, or inspiration care to cooperate. Stewart's newest novel, *Thornyhold,* was published in England and America in 1988.

Chapter Two
The Exploratory Novels: Instant Acclaim

Mary Stewart regarded her first few works as exploratory; she was experimenting with style, content, and point of view, but she wanted most of all to write a good story. Three of the novels discussed in this chapter are set in southern France, and the other takes place in Scotland on the Isle of Skye.

Madam, Will You Talk?

The first novel, *Madam, Will You Talk?* (1955), begins in Avignon and ends in Marseilles; Stewart once called this her "chase" story, not realizing at the time that the chase would become an important element in many of the stories. The plot of this novel involves episodes in almost a book-length flight and pursuit. Actually, only fourteen of the twenty-nine chapters (chapter 30 is a short epilogue) are part of the chase, which suddenly changes character midnovel with the protagonist now engaged in a pursuit of rescue. All along the way surprises and reversals appear, keeping high the level of suspense.

The protagonist, Charity Selborne, is a young English widow who has come to Avignon on vacation. There she meets a young boy, David, whom she befriends when guests at the hotel tell her that David's father, Richard Byron, an Englishman, has recently been acquitted of the murder of his best friend and of trying to kill his own son, who may have seen the murderer; this violence has come about supposedly over jealousy of Richard's beautiful second wife, who, it has been said, was having an affair with his best friend. The wife, Loraine, has fled to her native France with the boy and appears to be terrified of being found by Richard, who is stalking them.

Charity feels sorry for young David and invites him out for a day of sightseeing at a nearby town; while they are there, David's father appears. David, seeing his father from afar, hides in a church. Charity has been led to believe that Richard may be insane and that he intends to harm the boy. She therefore tries to mislead Richard. This is the beginning of the chase. Since this is a first-person narrative, the reader experiences Charity's fear and with her can only guess at the evil Richard is capable of.

After getting David safely back to Avignon, Charity leaves for the small town of Les Baux. The main part of the chase begins here, where Richard has followed and confronted her, wanting information about David. Charity fears for her life. What makes Charity an intriguing character, however, is that she is not a helpless female but an inventive, daring young woman—even if that daring is inspired by fear. The chase is made more equal, in fact, because she has acquired much experience and knowledge from her late husband, a race-car driver. Her car, a Riley, is fast, but Richard's car, a gray Bentley, is even faster and more powerful. The color is important because at various points in the auto chase Charity can gauge the pursuit and identify Richard's car.

When she first escapes from Richard, Charity temporarily immobilizes his car by removing the distributor cap and, by turning a screw, breaking the electrical contact—a trick, one learns, that young Britons used during World War II to keep people from stealing their cars.

Suspense mounts with each setback in the chase. Charity has a head start on the way to Marseilles, her present destination. The first setback occurs when she discovers she has taken the wrong road, the one across the river, and must backtrack and head east.

Later she is forced to wait at the river bridge in one-way traffic, and she spots the gray Bentley not far behind her. The next difficult situation comes at a train crossing. She is driving very fast and aggressively, racing the train toward the crossing. She blows her horn at the man in the sentry box, does not slow down, and barely makes the crossing as the bars crash down behind her.

Next she has a flat tire but pulls into a nearby bistro and garage. The proprietor can fix the tire and believes her invented story that her husband is following her and that she must elude him, she being on her way to join a lover in Marseilles. Richard does stop to ask if the proprietor has seen her car pass by, and the proprietor pretends he has seen it a half-hour before.

Charity waits for more than an hour before going on toward Marseilles. But Richard has not believed the proprietor, and close to the city she sees his car pulling out from the roadside trees and pulling in behind her. She is worn out by the chase and drives now as if Richard weren't there, but in the traffic, without trying, she loses him. She quickly puts the car into a parking garage and then walks toward the harbor and finds a hotel. Still later, avoiding the busy main street Canebiere, she joins a crowd gathered at the harbor for a sightseeing trip. Hoping to lose Richard completely, she remains at an island stop for more than an hour. She has seen Richard while she was waiting at the harbor but he was looking in the opposite direction; on the boat's return, now in the dark, she is dismayed to find him waiting for her.

The chase is over. She gives up now for whatever is to happen, but at this point the emphasis shifts. She finds now that Richard has been the victim, the target of several murder attempts when the original murder frame-up did not succeed. When Richard learned Charity was with his son, he assumed she was involved in the murder plot against him, an accomplice of his supposed wife and her real husband. Richard has pursued Charity to recover his son. One meets the handsome Frenchman, Paul Véry, Loraine's real husband, briefly at the Avignon hotel at the beginning of the novel. Both he and Loraine are in the employ of a smuggler/antique dealer, Kramer, who committed a crime while in the German army, a crime to which Richard and his friend were witnesses. At present Kramer cannot afford to allow anyone to know of his Nazi past.

Richard, also an antique dealer, is trying desperately to find out why he is being targeted. As he discovers that Charity has no part in the plot against him, he narrates the incidents of the past, and the two try to make sense of the mystery; they know only part of the answers.

All the major characters, including David, who has run away, are now in Marseilles with seemingly logical motives. In the next few hours both Richard and his son are drugged and abducted by Kramer and his people and are about to be murdered on a country road several miles from Marseilles. Charity, whose car is locked in the parking garage for the night, takes a ride from Paul Véry, embarking on a chase to save them. She has not known but soon discovers that Paul is one of the principals in the plot and that she too is about to become a victim.

A chase of sorts is an essential element of suspense in many of Mary Stewart's novels and is a life-or-death matter involving the female protagonist and, most often, a male villain whose intentions are to kill her. As in *Madam, Will You Talk?* part of the mystery lies in not being able to identify immediately the bad people; moreover, the heroine, through whose eyes we see these people, makes some serious but justifiable errors in judgment. Paul Véry is finally identified as the man responsible for the murders and an agent for the ex-Nazi Kramer. Mary Stewart does not flinch at involving her women characters in scenes of violence. Charity Selborne shows courage and physical bravery. She has tricked Paul Véry on the last chase and has gained control of the car. She is speeding and maneuvering the car, trying to make Paul lose balance and fall off it. They have arrived at the area where Richard and David have been taken. She sees the man Marsden, whom she mistakenly believes a part of the plot; he has a gun, and she heads the speeding car straight at him. He jumps aside but shoots at a front tire. A description of this tense moment follows:

There was a scarlet stab of flame: another. Then the car hit something, and the whole world heeled over in the rocketing, exploding skid. The Mercedes seemed to rear straight up in the air, and her headlights raked a dizzy arc of sky. Then they went out, and darkness stamped down on us as a man stamps on a beetle. Clinging to that crazily kicking wheel, blinded, half-stunned, wholly automatic, I fought the car. For a moment I thought I had her, then she swept into a bucketing turn. The night split, wheeled, hung suspended for a million years, then shattered into splinters of flame. Then silence, broken only by the tiny tinkle of falling glass.
There was a shout, a thud of feet running, the door of the Mercedes was wrenched open and hands seized me out of the darkness.[1]

Charity does not know that she is safe or that Richard has freed himself and David. Her car has ended almost at the edge of the cliff, from which there is a sheer drop to the sea. Paul has been knocked unconscious momentarily.

Coming behind them soon after is the Bentley with Kramer and Loraine, intent on completing their murderous business. Gaining consciousness, Paul Véry jumps into the Mercedes trying to warn them, but the car succeeds only in "plunging broadside on across the road," directly in the path of the oncoming car, which cannot avoid the crash. Stewart describes this fatal moment: "There was a yell, a dreadful scream, and then the cars met in a sickening crash of rending metal and shrieking tyres. . . . The cars hung there, black against the black sky, locked on the very brink of that awful cliff, then the beam swung over in a great flashing arc, and the locked cars dropped like a plummet down the shaft of light, straight into the sea" (*MWYT,* 169).

The ending is happy for the good people. Young David knows that the others have used him as a decoy to get his father. Marsden has been a Scotland Yard man all along, and Charity and Richard, who have already discovered their interest in each other, are now making plans to wed.

Aside from being a technique for suspense, the chase is a means of character development, showing the reader the true mettle of the principals, revealing in addition to courage their ingenuity, imagination, and determination. Charity does not behave like the stereotypical woman in distress, for although one experiences her terror and fears, one also sees her anger and her willingness to become involved, to say nothing of her talent for extricating herself from difficult situations.

In this novel Stewart demonstrates her ability to build a suspenseful plot. She understands people and presents believable motives for their behavior. The romantic element does not appear until the middle of the book, since Charity sees Richard only as someone to be feared; then, when they discover their interest in each other, the brief love scene does not interrupt the mystery and fast pace of the narrative.

Critics spoke of this first novel as "unusually skillful," "very promising," and written in "polished prose."

Wildfire at Midnight

Mary Stewart regards her second novel, *Wildfire at Midnight* (1956), as a classic closed-room detective story with restricted action and a larger-than-usual cast. The setting here is the Isle of Skye. This book, too, has a chase, but it comes nearer the end of the story, when the protagonist is running from the killer and trying to escape first in the fog on the riverbank and then into the hills.

The environment becomes an important part of the plot. The Cuillon Hills, composed of blue-black igneous rock rising sometimes to a height of three thousand feet, constitute a stark background. Tourists come mainly for rock climbing and fishing. Gianetta Drury, the main character, has come here, however, on vacation, as recommended by her family, for a much-needed rest.

The novel begins in Gianetta's home territory, London, where she is a model. In first-person narrative she provides family history and other relevant background information; with humor (and Stewart protagonists do have a sense of humor) she speaks of her notorious actress–great-grandmother, a raving beauty whom Gianetta apparently resembles; of her broken marriage to Nicholas Drury, a writer; and of her family in northern England—her father, a minister, and her spirited and charmingly absent-minded mother, who has not yet acknowledged Gianetta's divorce of four years.

The main characters congregate at the Camas Fhionnaridh Hotel on the island near the village of Elgol. More unusual among the vacationers is Marcia Maling, a beautiful young stage actress. In addition to the guests at the inn are the Gaelic-speaking villagers who assist as guides for the climbing and fishing activities.

The mystery has already begun two weeks before Gianetta's arrival: A young local girl has been murdered in a kind of sacrificial ritual on a bonfire, as was common in the early days of the islands when the natives worshiped other gods. It is believed that someone at the hotel is responsible, and the suspense begins as Gianetta receives warnings not to go about alone.

The introduction to the possible love theme comes early in this novel when Gianetta meets Roderick Grant, a young man who visits the area often and knows the island's culture and history. But the romantic situation is complicated, as one of the guests is Gianetta's ex-husband, Nicholas, whom she prefers to avoid, although she is obviously much affected by his presence. The beautiful actress, Marcia, causes friction, as she favors two of the guests, one of whom is Nicholas.

The real suspense begins with the disappearance of two climbers, Marian Bradford and Roberta Symes. Search parties finally find Marian Bradford's body with her climber's rope cut. While everyone is out in the hills, the body of one of the men of the searching party is found murdered and on a bonfire. Not until much later does Gianetta by chance discover Roberta Symes lying on a sheltered ledge, barely alive. Everyone knows by this time that a third, unknown climber, the murderer, had been with the women. Gianetta spends a hair-raising night as she (the only person not a suspect) looks after the unconscious Roberta, who can identify the killer. Although certain clues cause Gianetta to suspect her ex-husband, Nicholas, she does not tell the police what she has found.

The next afternoon, after professional medical and police aids have assumed responsibility for the care of the still-unconscious Roberta, Gianetta leaves for an appointed fishing lesson on the river. Precarious weather has been an important part of the atmosphere. As happens often, blinding mists develop. Gianetta's guide is attacked; a chase through the fog ensues. She hears Nicholas calling her, but she fears him now and over treacherous ground tries desperately to escape. Later she is relieved to discover Roderick Grant in a clearing as she reaches higher ground, but the reversal comes as Gianetta realizes (from a brooch she has found earlier) that Roderick is the guilty one, a schizophrenic, fanatic about (Celtic) worship of these mountains. Again Gianetta is forced to flee, climbing over the rocks upward into the hills with the murderer in pursuit. She is rescued by Nicholas and a search party. He, it turns out, has been in touch with her father and has come to the island, knowing she would be there.

The plot is immensely effective, and as in the other Stewart novels, description of the surroundings is a vital part of the fabric of the story; here the rocky, mountainous terrain is at the center of the action. As in *Madam, Will You Talk?* the heroine has been mistaken in her judgment of the villain, and as in any good mystery story the reader's views about the guilty parties undergo continual shifts.

Nicholas, like Richard Byron, is a mystery man, an unknown quantity, simply because the protagonist does not know his motives or the reasons for seemingly suspicious behavior, all of which are explained logically at the proper time. And in a mystery story timing is all, or almost all. Roderick Grant, the villain, is given a suitably emotionally unstable childhood, with much insanity in the family, twisted ideas about religion and nature, and a zealot's need to impress his views upon the world.

The villagers, such as Dougal Macrae, are good, wholesome, weatherworn people, adapted to the life of the water and the hills. Macrae has patience as he teaches Gianetta to fish, but he is also the fighting Scotsman, an angry bull breathing "fire and slaughter." It was his daughter who had been murdered and placed on the bonfire.

Gianetta, like Charity Selborne, is an immensely attractive character: She shows intelligence, courage, and compassion in addition to the spirit and determination of a fighter.

When Dougal Macrae is attacked in the mist so that Gianetta cannot see but can hear the thudding, gasping noise and then the silence, she says of herself: "I am not brave. I was horribly frightened, with a chill and nauseating terror. But I don't think anybody normal would unhesitatingly run away if they heard a friend being attacked nearby. . . . So I leaped forward, only to falter and trip before I had gone five yards, so blinding now was the mist that shrouded the moor."[2] In a few moments she has lost sense of direction, and now she knows the killer is nearby. The chase in its variations then goes on for four chapters, with Nicholas, in a final chapter, pursuing and subduing Roderick with the help of the other men.

The need to be "my brother's keeper" is part of the makeup of all of Mary Stewart's main women characters. Gianetta has divided loyalties; for the sake of truth and justice, she feels she must tell the police inspector the seemingly incriminating evidence against Nicholas, yet her attachment to him prevents her from doing so. She asks the inspector, "Has no one ever told you that people mean more to women than principles?" (*WM,* 139). She is distraught, but the inspector believes, one learns later, that she is withholding evidence to protect Roderick, whom he already suspects, not Nicholas. Roderick and Gianetta have been linked by the others as a "twosome."

Mary Stewart's "detective" story has been a success. In writing this book, she complained of the difficulty of keeping the characters confined and felt that plot was not one of her strengths. Her publishing history has shown otherwise. The plots of romance or suspense novels tend to be exaggerated, but plotting turns out to be one of Stewart's strengths.

In this novel Stewart identifies time (1953) by referring to two important events taking place in the outside world: the coronation of Queen Elizabeth and the conquering of Mt. Everest by Sir Edmund Hillary and a band of English climbers.

Thunder on the Right

Of all the novels, *Thunder on the Right* (1957) seems to be the one Mary Stewart dislikes the most. Actually, this novel was second in the writing but published after *Wildfire at Midnight*. Stewart once stated to Roy Lindquist in an interview that she would "like to see it drowned beyond recovery." She felt she had overwritten the book and had "splurged with adjectives, all colored purple."[3] This is the only suspense novel written from the third-person point of view, although one sees the world almost exclusively through the eyes of the protagonist, Jennifer Silver, a young English girl who is visiting a convent in southern France in the Pyrenees to meet her cousin Gillian, who is to be staying there.

In a town close by the convent, Jennifer is reunited with her friend Stephen Masefield, a music student studying abroad for two years; we already know that he is in love with Jennifer from their college days and that Stephen, like Nicholas in *Wildfire,* has been in touch with Jennifer's father, a music professor at Oxford, and has come to the area knowing Jennifer would be there. The pattern is different in this novel, however, since the background romantic friendship is established from the beginning and there is no confusion as to the innocent and the guilty characters. The big mystery involves cousin Gillian, whom Jennifer has not seen in several years, since Gillian has been living in France. Gillian's French husband has since died, and at this point in her life Gillian has decided to enter the convent at Gavarnie, first as a visitor to recover from an illness and then possibly to take orders as a nun. The idea disturbs Jennifer, and she has responded to Gillian's letter, written on the night three weeks previously, as Gillian was to leave Bordeaux to come to this area. An additional letter was promised but did not arrive.

Stephen acts as Jennifer's friend and confidant as she begins this venture and then becomes involved with her in solving the mystery. When Jennifer visits the convent, she is told that Gillian has died as the result of complications from an auto accident on the night of Gillian's arrival. The convent itself and especially one of the main officials—not herself a nun, Dona Francisca, a darkly mysterious, aristocratic Spanish lady and the main villain—have a negative influence on Jennifer. Jennifer is first horrified at the turn of events and then convinced that the lady buried in the convent cemetery is not her cousin. She is right. As events turn out, through more investigation by Jennifer, the reader learns that driving with Gillian on a mountain road on the night of the accident was a female fugitive, part of a smuggling ring. Taking Gillian's identification papers and leaving Gillian for dead, the fugitive made her way to the nearby convent, where she assumed Gillian's identity to avoid police arrest.

Pierre Bussac, a local mountain guide and smuggler of both people and goods into or out of Spain, has found the unconscious Gillian, now a victim of total amnesia, and nursed her back to health. He convinces Gillian that she is his wife, since he has become fond of her; she does not recognize Jennifer when they meet, and Pierre is ready for murder when he discovers who Jennifer is and that she is investigating (with Stephen) the smuggling involving Dona Francisca, who is receiving goods, mainly gold and art objects, at the convent but disguising the operation from the others. Since the Mother Superior is elderly and blind, the smuggling operation is not as difficult as it seems. Dona Francisca, who is blackmailing Pierre, insists that Gillian is a danger to them and must be eliminated, but Pierre will not give up Gillian.

In the final showdown, when Dona Francisca finds that the whole operation is being discovered, she stabs Pierre, intending to escape to Spain through the precarious, secret mountain shortcut used for the illicit trafficking. Pierre has sent Gillian ahead on the mountain trail to wait for him, but now, wounded, he enlists Jennifer's aid to warn Gillian and save her from Dona Francisca. The spectacular chase in the approaching darkness in the mountains has begun. A landslide, a rising cascade of water caused by a recent storm, and darkness complicate matters.

Pierre dies on the way, and Jennifer continues alone, trying to reach Gillian first and then hide with her until Dona Francisca has gone. But Dona Francisca appears, and Gillian flees in terror across a treacherous bridge of rock and Jennifer follows her. Gillian slips, falling a short distance; at this moment Stephen, who has previously gone for the police, appears and grapples with Dona Francesca. She stabs Stephen and in trying to stab him again loses her balance and falls to her death on the rocks below. The men from the village have arrived with Stephen but are farther back on the trail; Stephen must carry the unconscious Gillian and direct Jennifer back across the rocks that are now filling with water. When all is sorted out, Gillian's concussion has the effect of bringing back her memory, and she relates the events up to the accident but remembers nothing of the past weeks. Again, the ending is happy for the good people.

Jennifer is among the younger of the novels' protagonists (they range in age from twenty-two to twenty-seven); she is twenty-two, but she has the same spirit and courage as the others. Stephen is a music student and not the outdoor type; he has been wounded during the Korean War, which left him with a limp. Otherwise, he has about him a confidence, one is told, that ensures success. He is not the mystery man found in the two earlier novels, and he is not the dominant element in the resolution of the plot, being kept essentially in the background.

Nine Coaches Waiting

The fourth novel, *Nine Coaches Waiting* (1958), is the most complete and the best of the suspense novels. Critics have compared it with *Rebecca* and *Jane Eyre*. In all three novels the protagonist is an unworldly, rather defenseless young woman entering, as a governess (or companion), a world in which she does not belong but to which she becomes acclimated, partly through her own capabilities and charm and partly through the love of one of the central characters. Also, as in the story of Cinderella, with whom Mary Stewart's character compares herself, the protagonist falls in love with a prince charming and almost loses him in the mystery that follows. Indeed, the prince charming appears to be wicked.

In *Nine Coaches Waiting* the heroine is forced to believe through misleading evidence, as in *Madam, Will You Talk?* and *Wildfire at Midnight,* that the man she comes to love is a villain, guilty of murder or attempted murder.

Linda Martin, a lovely English orphan, comes to France to take the position of governess to nine-year-old Phillipe, the Comte de Valmy. He, too, has become an orphan at the death the previous year of his parents in an airplane accident. He has come from Paris, then, to stay with his Uncle Léon and Aunt Heloise while his guardian, Uncle Hippolyte, an archaeologist, is off for three months on a dig in Greece and Asia Minor. Young Philippe is actually the heir to the estate Valmy on which his uncle and aunt are living. Therein lies the problem.

Uncle Léon, during most of his life a vigorous, handsome, charming man, has, through an accident, become confined to a wheelchair. He still wields power and authority and delights in manipulating others. His son Raoul, living on a smaller estate at some distance from Valmy, has had a history of difficulty with his father. Their arguments are over money, one finds later, which his father draws from the smaller estate to use for the larger one.

Linda and Raoul fall in love, but from the beginning of her stay Linda senses contradictory elements in the behavior of Léon and Heloise and a marked antagonism between Philippe and his uncle. Several near accidents befall Philippe, and gradually Linda comes to realize that Philippe's uncle and aunt are trying to kill him.

The deed must be accomplished, Linda realizes, while Hippolyte is still in Greece. In fact, she has been engaged as governess because she is an orphan and has had no previous ties with her young charge. The former governess was apparently much attached to Philippe and was therefore dismissed. Because Linda has wanted the position, she has not indicated that she spent the first thirteen years of her life in Paris and so speaks French well and has understood more than Léon and Heloise are aware.

With each failed murder attempt suspense rises until there remains only one day before Hippolyte is to return home and resume custody of Philippe. This, then, must be the night of the murder. It appears now that Raoul, who has confessed his love for Linda, is in on the plot to kill Philippe. Moreover, the whole household and the neighboring townspeople now know that Raoul and Linda are unofficially engaged and, Linda finds later, if anything happens to the young boy, Linda herself may appear to have a motive to do away with him and be blamed for the murder if there is an investigation. She suddenly finds herself, therefore, a victim with Philippe. Has she been set up?

There is now conflict between Linda's love for Raoul, involving the need to trust him, and her duty to Philippe, requiring that she protect him from harm. Raoul has gone to Paris on the morning of that fateful day. Linda chooses duty, and in the night she and Philippe run away from the house to a small cabin across the valley in the woods. This belongs to an Englishman, William Blake, whom Linda has met several times in the village.

Now the big chase begins. The governess and her charge must stay out of sight until Hippolyte returns at midnight the next evening to his home in Thonon several miles away. Their absence from the chateau is quickly discovered that night, and the pursuit begins. Bernard, in Léon's employ, has, as Linda suspects, orders to find them and kill them.

One of the most suspenseful moments occurs when in the middle of the night Bernard comes into the cabin in which Linda and Philippe are hiding. They are lying in the loft, and Linda, hearing Bernard enter, believes this is the end. The next few moments are as follows: "I found that I was shaking, crouched together in my form of blankets. It wasn't the climb up the mountainside that had hurried Bernard's breathing and made his big hands clumsy on the lamp. It was excitement, the tongue-lolling excitement of the hound as it closes in. He knew we were here. He crossed the floor to the base of the ladder."[4]

But at the moment when Bernard seems about to climb the ladder, interruption comes by way of a villager doing night fire patrol, checking the dwellings in the area. Bernard admits he is looking for the missing governess and child and then leaves with the man, but Linda, shivering in the loft, is sure he will be back.

As soon as the men are gone, she awakens Philippe and they leave the cabin, heading through the forest in the direction of the town of Thonan, Hippolyte's home. They have taken some food with them and spend the rest of the next day and evening hiding in the fields and woods, progressing slowly toward their destination. They get a short ride from a farmer, and then at one point, while they are resting off the roadway, they see Raoul's car with Bernard slowly driving by, searching the countryside.

They end at eveningtime hiding in the boat house of Hippolyte's estate, from which they will emerge only when they are sure he has come home, yet when they think they are safe and at last enter the house, it is Raoul who is there. The shock is overwhelming, but then Hippolyte arrives almost immediately. The chase has covered fifty pages—five chapters—and kept the reader in exhilarating suspense.

Raoul, it seems, has discovered his father's evil plans and has threatened him if harm comes to either Linda or Philippe. Léon commits suicide, but even to the end the reader is in suspense as to Raoul's revenge against his father and his reaction to Linda's supposed lack of trust in him. Will Linda now turn to the young Englishman, Blake, who has come to her rescue following an urgent, mysterious telephone message sent him in the late afternoon? Not until the last page of the novel is the love story resolved, with the necessary communication and forgiveness bringing Raoul and Linda together.

Characterization in this novel is more complex and complete than in Stewart's other suspense novels. The autocratic Léon is a very real menace, a powerful personality. Heloise is equally threatening in her own icy, elegant way. She adores her husband and is willing to follow his commands to get what she believes should rightfully be his. She has the Lady Macbeth guilt complexes that cause her to walk in her sleep and deteriorate emotionally as she aids in the attempted foul play. She has poisoned Philippe's bedside chocolate drink, but as happens, he did not drink it.

Philippe is an entirely believable nine-year-old in a frightening situation: helpless, vulnerable from grief at the loss of his parents, fearful of his uncle but caring and trusting toward his young governess.

Raoul, like Nicholas in *Wildfire* and Richard in *Madam,* is a strong but mysterious character. His motives are unknown and his behavior is questionable. Linda does not want to believe him guilty, but she has Philippe to protect and she cannot risk being wrong. She, like the other heroines, is levelheaded, clever, a thoroughly decent human being, willing to risk her own life to protect, in this case, a child. She shows courage and determination in the process—also a sense of humor. For example, in an early chapter Linda and Philippe make an afternoon visit to the village and during this excursion Linda takes delight in teasing the apothecary who flinches at her schoolgirl French. She pretends she cannot speak "real" French, and he tries unsuccessfully to correct her:

I said gaily, in my most English French, "Oh, good morning Monsieur Garcin. It is a fine day, is it not? It was a fine day yesterday. It will be a fine day tomorrow. Not? I am looking at the soaps, as usual."

I said *par usuel,* and the chemist's thin lips pursed. It was his weekly pleasure to correct my French, always with that pained, crab-apple face, and I didn't see why I should deny him anything. (*NCW,* 46)

The household servants, too, have definite personalities. Of the friendly ones, the English housekeeper, Mrs. Seddon, is motherly, and although she, with her butler husband, has worked here thirty-two years, her French is apparently atrocious and adds a humorous touch. As far as Linda is concerned, Mrs. Seddon is the one normal and stabilizing element in the household. Linda says, "Mrs. Seddon . . . had all the trappings of the competent and superior housekeeper; but her voice and some of her mannerisms had, gloriously defying gentility, remained the homely and genuine voice and ways of Mary Seddon, erstwhile second-gardener's daughter." (*NCW,* 28).

Of the more important minor characters, there is William Blake, the young, athletic, kindhearted Englishman working in the area as a forester; although brotherly and protective, he might be, one feels, a willing candidate for Linda's affections.

In this novel, as in the others, description of the surroundings is effectively woven into the action, especially in the fields, hills, and woods of the chase. Mary Stewart more than most authors is at home in the out-of-doors and has ever-fresh means of presenting the natural elements. As Linda and Philippe have with difficulty crossed through the woods in the dark immediately after escaping from the house, near the area where the cabin should be, Linda observes:

If any other creature moved in the forest that night, we never saw it. The only eyes that glittered at us were the stars, and the million drops of stardew that shivered on the fallen boughs. The breeze was failing, and in its pauses the breaking of the dead stuff under our feet sounded like thunder. I found myself, absurdly, with a quick over-the-shoulder glance at Léon de Valmy's remote little light, trying to tread more softly, and eyeing in some dread the gaunt black shadows that the moon flung streaming down the open ride.

But no new terror waited under the swimming moon, and, when we stopped to rest, no sound came to us except the labored sound of our own breathing, and the age-old singing of the pines, and the rustle of wind-made showers as the dew shook down the boughs.

It was Phillipe who saw the hut. (*NCW,* 188–89)

In these lines, one sees less of Stewart the naturalist and more of Mary Stewart the poet.

Chapter Three
Mary, Queen of Hearts: More of Mystery and Suspense

Two of the novels discussed in this chapter take place in one of Mary Stewart's favorite areas of the world. She spent many happy hours in the sunny isles of Greece and on the mainland, enjoying the beauty of the land, the hospitality of the people, and the treasures of antiquity. *My Brother Michael* especially reflects her love of the literature of Greece in the novel's references to the writings of the great dramatists Euripides, Sophocles, and Aristophanes and its allusions to the culture and myths of that civilization. The chapter headings are often quotations from the plays. Mary Stewart and her characters know their classical literature. Both *My Brother Michael* (1960) and *The Moon-Spinners* (1962) have heroines who are temporarily in Athens; from there, the heroine of *My Brother Michael* journeys to the north to Delphi, while Nicola Ferris of *The Moon-Spinners* chooses the southern coast of Crete.

The third book included in this chapter, *The Ivy Tree* (1961), is more related to the much later novel *Touch Not the Cat* (1976); both books are set in England and represent definite departures from the pattern of the other suspense novels.

All these books have maintained their popularity. Indeed, F. W. J. Hemmings, in "Mary Queen of Hearts," *New Statesman,*[1] after two more novels had appeared, regretted that serious recognition had not been forthcoming and that the term *romantic* given often to Stewart's work was unfairly applied to these skillfully written, well-plotted novels. Most certainly in the narrow sense, "romance," a love interest, is never the major emphasis of the stories; in the background friendly and sometimes unfriendly relationships eventually evolve into a twosome.

These books, though, have no real love scenes, and at the finish of the adventure the leading male may do nothing more inflammatory than put a loving, protective arm around the lady. In fact, this final scene may be one of physical and emotional exhaustion, following a life-and-death struggle with a villain who has put up a good fight, so that with depleted energy, the concentration is more on "thanks be to

God that we've survived," rather than desire for a passionate love encounter. That is true also of the ending of *My Brother Michael*. Hemmings's article title, "Mary Queen of Hearts," an affectionate allusion
to Mary, Queen of Scots, also a Stuart, is not, then, so much that Mary
Stewart is the reigning monarch of the love story kingdom, as Barbara
Cartland might be, but that she reigns in the hearts of her readers, as
is evident from astronomic book sales. *My Brother Michael*, along with
The Ivy Tree and *The Moon-Spinners*, is often named among the favorites.

My Brother Michael

My Brother Michael (1960) is the story of Camilla Haven, a young
Englishwoman and a teacher in a girls' school; she, like most of Stewart's other protagonists, has been vacationing, but Camilla has been
touring the Greek islands and Crete. She would like now to go to
Delphi but is rather short of money. While she is in a café, almost by
magic a man delivers a key and tells her that the car for Delphi is
ready. It has been rented and paid for by a woman and is to be delivered
to a Monsieur Simon in Delphi. This is a matter of life and death, the
driver has been told. Camilla realizes that the situation must be a case
of mistaken identity, but after waiting futilely for some time for the
woman to show up, she finally takes the car, intending to deliver it to
Monsieur Simon when she gets to Delphi.

Thus begins a series of mysteries that extend throughout the novel.
In a small village close to Delphi, as Camilla is having problems maneuvering the car, she meets Simon Lester, an Englishman, also a
teacher of classics and also on holiday, except that his is a much grim-
mer mission. He is here to learn more about his brother Michael's death
on Mt. Parnassus near the end of World War II, fourteen years earlier.
Michael's last letter home indicated excitement over an important discovery but nothing more definite.

Camilla, with Simon's help, inquires in Delphi and the surrounding
area but cannot find anyone else named Simon. Simon Lester takes
Camilla with him as he visits the family that sheltered and then hid
his brother Michael during the German invasion. Stephanos, the elderly Greek head of the household, shows Simon where on Parnassus
Michael was murdered, not by the Germans but by Angelos, a Greek
ex-patriot turned renegade. Involved, one learns later, is a cache of
stolen British arms and gold, hidden in a cave during the war until
such time as Angelos could come back to claim it. Michael, it seems,

while in hiding discovered the cave and, in addition, a separate chamber concealing an unknown statue of Apollo, a seeming companion statue to the Charioteer. It was about this statue, apparently hidden centuries before, that Michael (also a classicist) was speaking in his letter.

For most of these fourteen years Angelos has been out of the country and incarcerated in Yugoslavia, but he has been in touch with his cousin Dimitrios in Delphi. One problem is that earthquakes have since altered the land formations in the cave area. Stephanos is now the only living person who knows the location of the murder, the end of which he witnessed, but is unaware of the hidden treasures nearby. Simon's visit and his questions about Michael's death have created much interest and prompted Dimitrios to have Simon followed in his expedition to the mountain with Stephanos. Camilla, present on these excursions, has already been involved in a minor night skirmish with Simon and a mysterious intruder (Angelos). By the end of the novel, Angelos, in his determination to retrieve the hoard, has murdered two people and is prepared to do away with Camilla; however, Simon appears in time to save her, and in the fight that follows, Angelos is killed.

Stewart's setting gives the reader an effective view of Delphi and its surrounding countryside in conjunction with the action involved; this is not simply a tourist-guide description. In addition, Stewart's descriptive passages here and in other works include details of the violent physical struggles, a realism not often found in novels by women writers. This more masculine treatment, along with Stewart's focus on suspense and action, may partly account for her popularity also with a male audience. She does not shy away from bloodshed. For example, in the final encounter on the mountainside, Camilla, already injured, sees Angelos backing, trying to get to the fallen gun as he and Simon confront each other. The narrative, as in the other novels, is in the first person:

Somehow I moved. It was like lifting a mattress stuffed with clay to lift my body from the scuffled dust, but I rolled over, kicked myself along the ground with one convulsive jack-knifing motion, like a fish, and grabbed at the dangling sleeve of the coat just as Angelos took a sudden, swift step aside, and stooped for the gun.

I had the sleeve. I yanked at it with all my strength. It caught at a bit of rock, tore, and came with a jerk. The torch flashed over like a rocket and crashed on a stone by my head. The gun flew high and wide, hit a pile of stones three yards away and slithered out of sight. It actually struck the Greek's hand as he reached to grab it. He whirled with a curse and kicked me and then went down sickeningly across the boulder as Simon hit him like a steam hammer.

Simon came in with a blow. The Greek's forearm, even as he went down over the rock, just managed to block the side-handed chop at the throat that followed it, and counter in the same movement with a wicked elbow punch that took Simon in the lower part of the stomach. I saw pain explode through him like a bursting shell, and as he recoiled the Greek, using the rock as a springboard, came away from it in a lunge with all his weight behind it. Simon's mouth disappeared in a smear of blood. His head snapped back in front of another blow that looked as if it had broken his neck and he went down, but as he went he hooked one leg round Angelos' knee and, using the man's own momentum, brought him crashing down over him. Before the Greek hit the ground Simon had rolled aside and was above him. I saw the Greek lash out with a foot, miss, and aim a short chopping blow with the edge of a hand at Simon's neck; Simon hit him in the throat and the two were locked, heaving and rolling in the dust that mushroomed up round them.

I couldn't see . . . couldn't make out. . . . Angelos was on his back, and Simon seemed to be across him, trying to fix the man's arm in a lock, to drag it under him as Angelos had dragged mine. The Greek smashed again and again at his face; the shortened punches hadn't much force behind them but the blood was running from Simon's mouth. Then suddenly the flailing fist opened, clawed, came down into Simon's cheekbone and slithered across it, the big spatulate thumb digging, digging, for his eye.[2]

Eventually Simon emerges the victor, and Angelos is dead.

Of the minor characters in the novel, notable is Nigel, a gawky young English artist who happened upon the cave and had made sketches of the statue of Apollo and of Angelos and Danielle. Danielle is a beautiful, ruthless young woman involved in a relationship with several people, including Angelos; it was she who rented the car in Athens. These are the two people whom Angelos murders, planning to leave their bodies in the cave until he can dispose of them. Camilla, hiding there, witnesses the murder of Danielle. The native Greeks, the elderly Stephanos, and his grandson Niko are authentic characters. The villainous Angelos, too, is believable in his greedy, cruel, bull-like behavior.

Once Simon has learned how Michael died, there is no mystery as to the identity of the villain, except that Angelos has been rumored dead. His appearance comes fairly late in the novel. Up to that point the focus has been on his cousin Dimitri, acting in Angelos's interests.

After the puzzle of Michael's death, the biggest mystery involves Michael's discovery, which turns out to be the priceless statue that Angelos has not seen but that Simon and Camilla, and Nigel before them, stumble on. Only they can appreciate the work of art enough to agree that it should remain in its hiding place, undisturbed.

After the big fight is a time of rest and explanations; the book ends as Camilla and Simon stand before the statue, which had been hidden from marauders perhaps two thousand years before, and present to Apollo a gold coin offering.

As mentioned earlier, the quoted chapter headings are capsule clues to the contents. Sometimes they create anticipation or are harbingers of conflict to follow; they may be warnings, but they are often humorous and always witty. For example, the heading for chapter 3 is from Aristophanes' play *The Frogs* and reads: "But if I don't get from under pretty damned soon, there'll be a disaster in the rear."[3]

In this chapter Camilla is in the hillside village of Arachova on her way to Delphi and is having trouble maneuvering the strange car, for the street is only eight feet wide and she has met a truck. She is the one, however, who has to back up, and that causes problems. The whole male population of the village is enjoying the spectacle: "Eventually I reversed it into somebody's shop doorway. The whole village helped to pick up the trestle table, rehang the rugs, and assure me that it didn't matter a scrap. I straightened up the car and reversed again, into a donkey. The whole village assured me that the donkey wasn't hurt and it would stop in a kilometre or so and come home" (*MBM,* 27).

Behind her now is a curve with a 20-foot drop, but help comes from Simon, who then drives with her to Delphi.

The Ivy Tree

With *The Ivy Tree* (1961) Mary Stewart for the first time comes to home territory: Her protagonist arrives from Canada by way of Newcastle to visit northern England, the home of her ancestors. The heroines of the suspense novels thus far have been young women visiting most often a foreign land. In this respect, Mary Grey, the central character of *The Ivy Tree,* almost fits the established pattern; she is a visitor, but here there is no crime to be solved. There is nothing unusual about the house or the estate of Whitescar; no smuggling of gold or jewels; no murder; no real battle scene, although an act of violence almost occurs at the end of the story; no spectacular chase, although Mary

must race for help to save the lives of the two men trapped in the caved-
in gate house.

Yet *The Ivy Tree* is one of the most suspenseful of the novels, a mas-
terpiece of reader manipulation. It is the story of an impersonation.
When Connor Winslow sees Mary Grey and mistakes her for Annabel
Winslow, he realizes the benefits to him if she could come to live at
Whitescar, where he is the manager, and pretend to be the long-lost
Annabel. Annabel, an orphan, has left her home eight years before and
has been presumed dead, but as a favorite of her elderly grandfather,
who owns the farm, she, along with a youthful cousin named Julie,
would be an heir to the property. Connor (Con), a more distant relative, has been working on the farm for years and hoping to inherit it,
but the grandfather, now quite ill, is obstinate enough not to let anyone know how he intends to divide the property and money; furthermore, he refuses to believe that Annabel is dead.

Mary Grey, now working at a café in Newcastle, succumbs to the
persuading of Connor and his sister Lisa, housekeeper at Whitescar,
and agrees to play the role of Annabel. After three weeks of intensive
preparation and drilling, Mary comes to Whitescar as the long-lost
Annabel.

Much of the suspense is created by the uncertainty of the situation
and the emotional strain Mary Grey undergoes to keep from being
discovered. She has agreed with Con that whatever she gains from an
inheritance will be passed over to him; a contract of sorts is made
between them.

Complications arise when Mary meets Adam Forrest of the adjoining
estate, the man with whom Annabel had been in love. At the time,
Adam was married to a psychically unbalanced alcoholic who later accidentally set fire to their house. Adam saved his wife but was severely
burned in the process. After a quarrel with Adam eight years before
and pressure from her grandfather to marry Con, Annabel had run
away, sending a message later from America that she would never
return.

In a twilight encounter with Adam, Mary tells him that she is not
Annabel; he threatens to expose her and her and Con's scheme if anyone
is hurt by it.

Julie, the young and lovely cousin, arrives for a short stay and is
informed that the grandfather is seriously ill. She is accompanied by a
friend, an archaeologist, who is working on the excavation of Roman
ruins a few miles away. Mary seems to be doing a creditable job of

convincing everyone that she is indeed Annabel, but even after the first day she begs Con to let her out of their agreement so that she can leave. He will not do so, however, and convinces her to stay. Conflicts with Con arise, and his behavior seems increasingly desperate and erratic. The grandfather tentatively confides to "Annabel" that he is thinking of leaving the property to Con but most of the money to her and Julie.

Fairly late in the novel (chapter 14 of eighteen), the reader is shocked to learn that Mary Grey is indeed Annabel, wanting to keep hidden her real identity for personal reasons. Adam Forrest discovers the truth when Annabel, under stress one evening, takes his horse Rowan for a midnight ride. Mary Grey had claimed ignorance of horses, but Annabel was said to be a whiz with them. Only a few words are exchanged between them, and Annabel insists their relationship has ended. She tells Adam that aside from her quarrel with him on that night long ago, she had feared for her life since Con, in a fury, tried to kill her.

On the same afternoon that the grandfather dies, a further crisis develops; in a storm, lightning strikes the old ivy tree and it splits, falling on the adjoining gate house, causing the roof to cave in and trapping Julie's archaeologist friend, Donald Seton; Adam tries to free him and stays with him to keep him from bleeding to death. Con tries desperately to shore up the walls but needs help and equipment. Telephone service is out. It is at this point that Annabel makes a harrowing quest for help, traveling over back roads, fields, and a river crossing, first by car and then on horseback. She reaches a neighboring family, who come with help.

But as the final rescue operations are taking place, Con, who has left that scene, comes to confront Annabel in the stable as she tends to Rowan after her wild ride for help. Con is aware now of her real identity. Jealousy, anger, and frustration at the vulnerability of his situation cause him to make a movement of attack, at which she screams and jumps away; the horse, rearing, strikes Con and kills him. Adam arrives just after this happens; he and Annabel realize they must not waste any more of their lives by remaining apart.

Perhaps because one knows them better, the characters in this novel are more satisfactory and seem more complete than those in many of Stewart's other suspense novels. One has these characters' histories—what they were before and what they are now, eight years later.

Connor Winslow is an ambiguous character. One sees him as a

charming Irishman, handsome, hardworking, and unappreciated but also single-minded and ruthless, and even from the beginning one receives hints of the violent streak. Yet he is sympathetic enough so that the reader suspects he may become Annabel's partner by the end of the novel, an outcome that would solve the inheritance problems. It is difficult to think of him as a villain.

His half-sister Lisa is a plain, silent young woman but older than Con and devoted to him. She is kept in the background.

Adam Forrest one knows less about, since he appears very little in the novel; one does know from hearsay that he has suffered for years in an unhappy marriage and has taken his wife to the Continent for cures and treatment at various institutions, living abroad for most of the past eight years. She has eventually committed suicide. As a result of the fire and the destruction of the house, Adam's hands are badly scarred and the family coffers depleted. Adam reminds one of Jane Eyre's Mr. Rochester. He senses from Annabel's reaction to his wounds that she still has deep feelings for him, yet he did not receive her final letter, years before, stating a continued pledge of love and a willingness to go off with him. She, of course, then received no reply, and the ending for both was therefore abrupt and painful.

One of the most interesting people in the book is Julie's Scottish friend Donald Seton. (One suspects that he may resemble Mary Stewart's own husband.) He is reserved and solemn, yet kind and warmhearted. It is his exploring the heretofore-undiscovered Roman stones in the old gate house that almost costs him his life when the crushed roof pins him underneath.

The grandfather is a cantankerous old man, afraid to give up his power and allow others to know his plans. Con finds his lack of praise particularly frustrating, for Con does his best to make a success of the farm. The old man sincerely loves Annabel and Julie, however, and does appreciate Con, although he never says so. It has been his hope that Con and Annabel will marry so that the estate will remain intact.

Julie is a more conventional, stereotyped character. In her early twenties, she is attractive and has an interesting life in London working for the BBC. Her share of the property is not important to her, for her own family situation guarantees her a suitable income and she has no desire to live at Whitescar. Donald is different from Julie's previous friends, and she is delighted when he finally proposes.

Annabel's character borders on the mysterious. Though the reader shares her thoughts and emotions, those thoughts are focused on the problems of the present. There are brief references to the past only when one finally knows her as Annabel. One knows very little of her life or whereabouts for the past eight years. She has been caring for an invalid in Canada, near Montreal, she says, and then at her employer's death, six months before, has decided to return to England; having little money, she begins working in the café in Newcastle, hoping for a chance to see about the inheritance due her from her mother. She is wary of Con, one learns eventually, and goes along with the impersonation scheme to protect the interests of her grandfather and Julie and to see them once again. She shares the positive characteristics of Stewart's other leading characters.

What is most remarkable about Annabel's character, however, is the skill with which Stewart presents her thoughts and emotions without betraying the secret that she is really Annabel and not Mary Grey. There are no false notes. Her reactions are entirely suitable and reasonable for her situation as the impersonator. Then, when she reveals herself as the real Annabel, the reader has been wholly taken in, having found "Mary's" behavior as believable as it is when she assumes her real identity. Her character is consistent and convincing, an amazing feat.

The tone of this book is much more subdued and serious than that of Stewart's other suspense novels. Some critics have suggested that the ending might in fact have been more meaningful without the happy resolution of the love affair; however, given the storybook situation, the ending seems appropriate. The literal ending comes full circle with the beginning. The novel opens with Mary Grey/Annabel sitting on the rock formation of Hadrian's Wall, daydreaming, when suddenly Con appears and disturbs her thoughts. At the end she has come here again to sit in peace and quiet and to forget the recent traumatic events. As she sits musing, Adam appears and she quietly takes his hand in hers:

Though I had been waiting, I hadn't heard him approach. He had come quietly along the turf to the south of the Wall. He was standing close behind me. The lambs, sleepy-eyed, had not even raised their heads.

I didn't turn. I put up a hand, and when his closed over it, I drew the scarred back of it down against my cheek, and held it there.

Time is to come. . .

—The End—[4]

There is no passionate love scene, only quiet acceptance of the relationship.

Titles of the Stewart novels are not always readily identifiable with the contents of the story, but here in *The Ivy Tree*, the tree itself is a major landmark on the estate and becomes a central character in several ways. It had been used formerly as a post office, a receptacle for letters between Adam and Annabel in their secret romance. The last letter sent by Annabel to Adam had been put into the opening of the tree by the young Julie, who discovers their secret and assumes Adam will receive it there even after Annabel has gone. Of course he doesn't, and now after the storm, Julie and Annabel find the letter in the broken tree, still sealed, as it has been for eight years. Ironically, Julie apologizes and hopes that it wasn't important, but Annabel realizes now that it was better that Adam did not receive it.

The stroke of lightning and the fallen tree precipitate the near-fatal accident as the tree crashes into the gate house. This crisis forces the emergency that follows, including the confrontation leading to the death of Con. Annabel has referred to the ivy tree as symbolic of the past of deceit and lies.

If one were to search for symbolism in the names of the characters, perhaps one should have realized from the beginning that a man called Con is likely to be deceitful and disarmingly clever, while anyone named Adam is bound to be the survivor and the one to end up with the girl.

The Moon-Spinners

The latest paperback edition (eighteenth printing, 1986) of *The Moon-Spinners* (1962) is labeled as "A dramatic chase through the savage Greek countryside."[5] That rugged territory is the White Mountains of Crete, the supposed birthplace of Zeus. Crete's ancient Minoan civilization reached advanced stages, and Homer spoke of more than a hundred cities in ancient Crete. Modern Crete, however, has only three major urban areas, all on the northern coast.

Mary Stewart's protagonist, Nicola Ferris, has preferred to visit the southern coast and to spend her Easter holiday in the little village of Agios Georgios (St. George), a rather primitive hamlet in which a small hotel is just opening. Nicola is the first guest; her cousin Frances, much older, is on a cruise with friends and is to be joining Nicola there.

The novel begins with the sighting of an egret and Nicola's excitement at exploring the beauties of the area as she wanders about the mountainside in pursuit; she has just arrived and is making her way from the main road, downward in the walk, to the village. The opening paragraph is another fine example of Stewart's power of description, at the same time hinting of the extraordinary and the danger in the background:

It was the egret, flying out of the lemon-grove, that started it. I won't pretend I saw it straight away as the conventional herald of adventure, the white stag of the fairy tale, which, bounding from the enchanted thicket, entices the prince away from his followers, and loses him in the forest where danger threatens with the dusk. But, when the big white bird flew suddenly up among the glossy leaves and the lemon-flowers, and wheeled into the mountain, I followed it. What else is there to do when such a thing happens on a brilliant April noonday at the foot of the White Mountains of Crete; when the road is hot and dusty, but the gorge is green, and full of the sound of water, and the white wings, flying ahead, flicker in and out of deep shadow, and the air is full of the scent of lemon-blossom? (*MS, 9*)

But danger there is, and Nicola does not make it to the village that night. She is confronted by a menacing man with a knife and then meets, in a shepherd's hut close by, his companion, a young Englishman, Mark, who is suffering from a gunshot wound—all this because Mark and his younger brother Colin have witnessed a murder while sightseeing on the mountain. Colin has been taken prisoner, and it was thought that Mark had been killed as he fell some distance after being hit. Lambis, the Greek with the knife, has been their guide, taking them from island to island in his boat: The day of the misfortune was their first on the island of Crete. Lambis had waited with the boat and then, searching for the brothers, found Mark lying wounded.

Mark remembers that three men and one woman were at the scene of the crime. One of them, a swarthy man in Cretan dress, is now hunting him in the hills and rocks, with intent to kill. Although Mark and Lambis want Nicola to leave and not get involved, she insists on staying with the feverish Mark while Lambis goes back to the boat at dusk for medical supplies and food. The two men also want desperately to get some word of Colin, whether he is still alive—and if so, where he has been hidden—or if he has come back to the boat.

The next morning, when Lambis has not returned, Nicola and Mark seek another, less obvious hiding place on a ledge higher up, covered by underbrush. Nicola washes the wound and shares what is left of her own knapsack of food. They then see the Cretan coming, carrying a rifle and field glasses. He searches the hut and comes close to their spot but goes on. Suspense is increased because Nicola and Mark don't know who the guilty people are or whether they are from the village.

Nicola, having promised to be careful, goes down to the village, collecting her suitcase left in the bushes under a bridge the day before. The proprietor of the hotel, Stratos, is a Cretan who has lived in London for the past twenty years and is now back in his native village. With him is an associate, Tony, an Englishman who is to help with their four-bedroom hotel. Stratos has a sister, Sofia, who is helping at the hotel but lives in the village with her Turkish husband, Josef. These four turn out to be the villains; Josef is the killer, and Sophia tries to protect Colin from being murdered also.

Once in the village, Nicola, as unobtrusively as possible, conducts a search. Almost immediately she comes to suspect Stratos and the others but must appear unknowing and uninvolved. Nicola's search for Colin occupies the next six and a half chapters, and indirectly help comes from her cousin Frances. The hunt is frustrating and often close; by accident Nicola and Frances come upon the particular windmill in which Colin has been kept prisoner but from which he has just been freed by Sophia. Mary Stewart is as expert in the plotting of the hunt as she is in the manipulation of the chase, with consistently tense moments as Nicola here runs the risk of being discovered.

Eventually Nicola does find Colin, and they are reunited in secret with Mark and Lambis. Josef, the Turk, has been killed in an encounter with Lambis, and the three young men plan to leave immediately in their boat for Athens to contact the authorities. They designate a night rendezvous should Nicola and Frances decide to leave with them.

By now Stratos is almost certain of Nicola's involvement, Josef is missing, and the situation has become critical. Nicola and Frances leave the hotel in the night, planning to send to the boat in the bay the light signal agreed upon. They must walk some distance on the rough ground of the rocky shore before coming to the cove.

A series of setbacks occurs. There is no moon, for which they are grateful, but in the blackness Frances sprains her ankle, the flashlight breaks, and the cigarette lighter gets wet. Now they cannot signal. They believe they see the boat. Nicola sheds her outer clothing and attempts to swim toward the boat. After some confusion she hears another boat and swims toward it. It is Stratos's boat. He puts on his spotlight and is convinced, one finds later, that Nicola is stealing the jewels anchored by the rocks in a special container. Twice he throws harpoons at her and tries to run her down. She is hurt, but then Mark's boat rescues her. She seems to have been pulled down by a net, which turns out to be the one holding Stratos's stolen jewels. One learns later that Stratos and Tony have been receiving stolen goods from robberies in London; the murdered man was an accomplice. This scene in the water, representative of the physical confrontation that Stewart's heroines often undergo, showing their physical courage and stamina, is played out in an entirely believable way.

The last chapter—the tying up, the squaring with the village elders, and the explanations—is naturally anticlimactic, and if the dialogue and mood seem a bit too lighthearted, perhaps part of this can be forgiven by the age of the participants: Mark (Nicola as well) is only twenty-two, and he seems to view this experience as an adventure, being in that respect somewhat like Conrad's young Marlow in the story "Youth." Although no love scene develops, the interest is there and one knows that Nicola and Mark will get together.

Reference to the legend of the moon-spinners comes up several times in the novel. Nicola tells Mark the story on that first night in the shepherd's hut. The moon-spinners are water nymphs who on their spindles spin the moon down out of the sky. Each passing night the moon gets smaller until it is gone and then the world is in darkness, keeping the creatures of the hillside safe from the hunter. On the darkest night they wash their wool in the sea; from the spindles the wool unravels from the shore to the horizon and the moon rises again from the sea. When all the wool is wound again in a ball in the sky, "the moon-spinners start their work once more, to make the night safe for hunted things" (*MS*, 55). In this case, Mark, Colin, and Nicola are the hunted things.

As in most of the other novels, one learns very little about the characters. Nicola has been a secretary for a year in the British embassy in Athens, but her thoughts in the story are almost entirely on solving the problems at hand; aside from perhaps having greater interest in the wildlife and plants of the region than some of Stewart's other protagonists, Nicola shows the same concerns and positive qualities of the other Stewart women. All the "good" people have a strong moral sense, a belief in an honorable world. They are not cynical, and for them life continues to be an adventure.

Although sharing the same title, the movie of *The Moon-Spinners*, starring Hayley Mills, bears little resemblance to the book. Major changes were made that could not duplicate the narrative excitement of the book. Nicola's character was made much younger; Frances's role was enlarged; the plot involving Mark was changed; Colin, Lambis, and Josef were eliminated; new characters were added; and the illegal jewel ring was expanded to involve the ambassador and an eccentric British woman on a yacht. Even the setting was altered: The quiet, primitive village was transformed into a lively fiesta resort. One can only hope that Mary Stewart did not see the movie; she would not have been amused.

Chapter Four
This Rough Magic
and the Later Novels

This Rough Magic (1964) is more closely allied to *The Moon-Spinners* and *My Brother Michael* than to the other novels discussed in this chapter in that it, too, has a Greek setting—but in the Ionian Sea, on the island of Corfu. *Airs above the Ground* (1965) takes place in Austria and *The Gabriel Hounds* (1967) in Lebanon in the days when Lebanon was still a land to visit; *Touch Not the Cat* (1976), the much later novel, returns to northern England, and although it was published after the first Arthurian works, *The Crystal Cave* (1970) and *The Hollow Hills* (1973), it belongs with the suspense stories and is most closely allied to *The Ivy Tree*.

This Rough Magic

This Rough Magic receives its title from Prospero's speech in *The Tempest* (act 5, scene 1), in which he is about to give over his magical presence, "drown" his book of wizardry, and say good-bye to his island. This is the same speech that certain scholars have suggested might have been Shakespeare's own farewell to the theater. Prospero says, "But this rough magic / I here abjure, and, when I have requir'd / Some heavenly music, which even now I do, / To work mine end upon their senses that / This airy charm is for, I'll break my staff, / Bury it certain fathoms in the earth, / And deeper than did ever plummet sound / I'll drown my book."[1]

Aspects of the play *The Tempest* are not only part of the background of this novel but also involve certain elements of characterization and plot. To begin with, Corfu is often thought of as the island Shakespeare had in mind when he wrote *The Tempest*. In *This Rough Magic* Julian Gale, a retired actor, tells Lucy Waring, the protagonist, that he too believes this theory and gives several good reasons for doing so, among them points dealing with the location, the terrain of the island, the mountains, the caves, the brine pits, the lime trees, and the other kinds of vegetation mentioned in the play. Prospero, the father figure and magician who controls the island, may well have been inspired by the story of Saint Spiridion, whose body was brought to the island in 1489 and who had a reputation for all sorts of magic, weather magic in particular. Four times each year, his body is paraded through the streets of the village of Corfu; moreover, brought with him to Corfu was a female saint who is treated as a lesser figure and not given the same adulation, a possible model for Prospero's daughter Miranda.

As *This Rough Magic* opens, Lucy Waring, a young English actress at present unemployed, has come to spend some time with her sister Phyllida (Phyl) Forli, who is married to an Italian banker with a family home on Corfu. While there, Lucy meets Julian Gale, the retired actor whom she has admired for years in the British theater, and his son Max, a musician currently composing the score for a film version of *The Tempest*. She also meets Godfrey Manning, an English author-photographer.

Working for Manning is Spiro, a young Greek boy whose twin sister, Miranda, is employed in Phyllida's household. They are Julian's godchildren. Julian, who knew their father, has been coming to Corfu for years. Soon after the novel opens, Spiro is reported missing, having fallen off the Manning boat in a night sailing. Because of the island's proximity to Albania, several of the local people are involved in minor smuggling operations. In the north, Corfu is only two miles off the Albanian coast, but no legal dealings are possible with that country.

Several suspicious events occur, including the murder of a young Greek man. Lucy suspects that Max Gale is responsible for some of these evils, but as occurs in other Stewart novels, the heroine suspects the wrong man. Halfway through the book, the secret reappearance of Spiro, retrieved from the Albanian coast at night by Max, alerts Lucy to the fact that Godfrey Manning tried to kill Spiro by hitting him over the head and dumping him overboard. Only the Gale household and Lucy know this information; Spiro's presence and the trips that he, accompanied by Max, makes to Athens to both the hospital and the police must be kept secret from everyone else, especially Manning. The rest of the book is then devoted to sidetracking Manning and trying to find out what kind of secret operation he is involved in. Lucy at one point is delegated to keeping him out of the way while Max arrives bringing Spiro back from Athens. Setbacks occur along the way, keeping reader tension at a high level.

One of the problems is that the police, on the word of Spiro alone and with no other evidence, will not consider taking action against Manning. Proof of wrongdoing must be obtained. Leading to this in a roundabout way is a discovery made by the young people, Miranda and her fiancé, Adoni, who believe they may have found the actual book of magic that the legendary Prospero of *The Tempest* threw away ("drowned")—this in a deep cave and down a shallow well near Manning's house. The two have grown up with Julian Gale's story of Prospero; when Miranda excitedly reports the discovery, Lucy asks to see the cave and the book.

Lucy and Miranda go by night (most of the activities seem to occur at night), and with the help of a flashlight Lucy sees in the water the half-hidden object, which might have looked like a big book but is a sturdy waterproof box. They hear someone coming and hide; they then see Manning with a grappling hook retrieve two boxes, carrying them one by one to his boat house. When Manning drives away in his car, Lucy searches both the boat house (Miranda knows where the key is hidden) and the boat to find the boxes; however, just as she hauls one aside to look at the contents, Manning returns. Dropping the box into the water, Lucy hides in the cabin but is forced to reveal herself shortly after the boat is at sea. Although the attractive Godfrey Manning has been one of the possible love interests earlier in the novel, no love is lost now as he freely admits he has been running shipments of forged currency to Albania on behalf of two neighboring countries to cause the collapse of the current government; Greece will be blamed. This is the last shipment, and he will leave Corfu almost immediately.

After an angry scene, Manning tries to choke Lucy, but with the aid of the sailboat's sudden movements and the swinging boom, she evades him; in the scuffle she purposely kicks the throttle open just before Manning fires a shot at her, and she jumps into the water. A ship's light not far away keeps him from searching for her. She gets to shore eventually, exhausted but aided at the very end by a boost from the tamed dolphin that earlier in the novel she and Max had rescued on the beach. On the surface, the action here sounds impossible and implausible, but Mary Stewart's description and narrative make the events entirely believable, for one experiences both Lucy's terror and her determination to survive.

Several hours later, when Lucy returns to Manning's house, the police and everyone else are there confronting Manning. He breaks away and, after a fight with Max, escapes to his boat. As he starts the engines, however, the boat explodes: Adoni had turned on the gas jets in the cabin, just in case Manning tried to leave. The box of forged currency Lucy earlier dropped into the water is evidence enough for the authorities to understand the seriousness of Manning's illegal activities.

As these traumatic events are ending, Max proposes marriage and Lucy accepts but in no private romantic love scene. Julian Gale has determined to give up his retirement and (like Prospero) go back—in his case, to the London theater and possibly a role, but not that of Prospero, in their film version of *The Tempest.*

As suspicious as Max Gale has appeared in the beginning of the story, one begins to change one's view of him when he helps Lucy rescue the beached dolphin, discovering the truth thereafter about his unusual behavior. And as charming and attractive as Godfrey Manning has seemed at the beginning, he is convincing as the dispassionate killer he turns out to be.

Phyllida serves as a contrast to her sister Lucy. She is the wealthy young matron, occupied with her own affairs and on the periphery of the action, never quite knowing or being told what is going on.

Miranda, Spiro, and Adoni are warm, attractive, wholly likeable young people, simple and good. It is obvious from Stewart's handling of the Greek characters in her books that she admires and respects them. If the villains are Greek, they are unusual. Of the villains in the Greek stories, Josef in *The Moon-Spinners* is a Turk whom the Greeks themselves despise, Tony is an Englishman, and Stratos is a Cretan corrupted by twenty years in London. Angelos of *My Brother Michael* is treated as an outcast by his own compatriots, who are ashamed of him. And, of course, Manning in *This Rough Magic* is an Englishman.

All the chapter headings of *This Rough Magic* are lines from the play *The Tempest* and are apt for the events therein. For instance, the rescuing of the beached dolphin takes all of chapter 9; in the dark, with the help of Max's boat just after he has rescued Spiro from the Albanian coast, Lucy and Max finally get the dolphin back into the water. The lines heading this chapter are Prospero's words to Ariel as he frees him at the end of the play. Here, they apply to the dolphin: "To the elements / Be Free, and fare thou well!"[2]

Airs above the Ground

Mary Stewart seems to love animals, and she obviously knows a great deal about horses and riding. This talent is apparent in *The Ivy Tree* in

Annabel's ability to handle horses and is even more obvious in Stewart's choice of Austria and the Lipizzan Stallions as the background for *Airs above the Ground* (1965). Her visits to Vienna and to the Spanish Riding School were the inspiration for the plot of *Airs above the Ground*. Its protagonist is Vanessa March, a young veterinarian who has treated horses and whose father was also a veterinarian to a stable of racehorses.

This is one of Stewart's major "chase" novels, beginning with a quiet pursuit of a missing husband and, for almost the last half of the book, involving three continuous but separate chases.

The story begins in London with a mystery. Vanessa's husband of two years, Lewis, has supposedly gone to Stockholm on business, but a friend's information prompts Vanessa to see a newsreel about a circus fire in a small village in Austria. In the film she sees Lewis in the background and next to him a lovely blond girl.

In chapter 2 Vanessa is on the plane to Vienna to investigate the mystery of Lewis. Accompanying her is a friend's seventeen-year-old son, Timothy, who is to visit his father in Vienna. On the trip Timothy expresses his interest in the Lipizzan Stallions and in the Spanish Riding School, where he hopes to find a job. The Vienna visit with his father does not work out, and Timothy asks to go with Vanessa to Oberhausen, the village of the circus fire. Two men have died in the fire: One was Franzl Wagner, cousin of the circus owner, and the other, Paul Denver, a visiting Englishman. Vanessa and Timothy meet the blond girl of the newsreel, Annalisa Wagner, who, with her father, manages the circus. They then meet Lee Elliot, another Englishman, who was supposed to contact Paul Denver but arrived too late to do so; Elliot aided in the rescue of the animals when the fire started and helped care for the horses in the critical days that followed. Not until chapter 8, when Lee Elliot makes a secret night visit to Vanessa, does the reader discover that he is really Lewis March, her husband. He has pretended not to recognize her earlier and she has responded in like fashion to his sign, but she has no idea why. It turns out that he is on a secret mission; aside from his regular job, he has also been working as a secret service agent.

Becoming involved with the circus too, Vanessa performs surgery on one of the old piebald horses injured in the fire, the favorite of the deceased Franzl Wagner. This horse turns out to be a Lipizzan Stallion, stolen by Franzl from the national training farm where Franzl had been working ten years before. Franzl then joined the circus, changed his

name, and used patches of dye to disguise the horse. On his deathbed
Franzl spoke insistently about the horse's saddle, but his message
seemed to make no sense.

Vanessa and Timothy go off to a new village with the circus while
Lewis, still as Lee Elliot, reports to Vienna. Vanessa and Timothy tell
the Wagners what they have learned about the stolen horse. Annalisa
has found the old newspaper clippings and the dye. Since the horse is
now of no use to the circus, Vanessa suggests that she take him and
return him to the Spanish Riding School; the Wagners agree and give
her the big old saddle stitched with imitation jewels that Franzl used.
The circus is ready to leave for Yugoslavia and will not return for several months.

The villain of the story is Sandor Balog, a properly satanic-appearing
high-wire artist. When he discovers that Vanessa has been given the
saddle, he pays her a night visit in the castle-inn (Schloss Zechstein)
where she is staying. He orders her to get the saddle, which she has
deposited in the corn bin of the elaborate old stable. For some time
the reader and Vanessa think the jewels may be the desired objects,
but no. During the scene of threats and semiviolence, Vanessa manages
to slip out and get to the turrets and roof of the castle. Sandor chases
her. This happens in chapter 14; for the last eight chapters of the book,
chases that change character and direction occur almost continuously,
maintaining a breathless pace and the utmost of suspense.

In this first chase, Vanessa finally escapes and hides in a carriage in
the stable. Lewis has arrived but stays out of the way, hoping to follow
Sandor Balog to his contacts. Sandor locates and then tears apart the
saddle, taking out packages that are later discovered to be cocaine.
Once Sandor leaves, Lewis, with Vanessa and Timothy, follows him at
high speed down the mountainside, yet keeping a careful distance,
through a town and up another mountain containing a railway and a
restaurant at the top. The last part of the pursuit has to be on foot.

Sandor meets his contacts, the Beckers, who are the proprietors of
the restaurant and linked to others in Vienna. Lewis surprises them
and there follows a violent battle in which Vanessa and Timothy also
become entangled, until Sandor and the Beckers are subdued. Vanessa
and Timothy rush down the mountainside for help, but first they are
to retrieve the packets of cocaine from the split tree where they saw
Sandor hide them. In the process of doing so, Timothy falls, slides,
and lands with a twisted broken leg upon the railroad track, his foot
jammed under a tie of the cogwheel track.

After trying unsuccessfully to free him, Vanessa gets into the car, speeding down to the small railroad depot for help. Most of this action has taken place at night, and now it is almost morning. The reader knows that a 7:00 A.M. sightseeing train will be coming up the mountain, but when Vanessa gets to the depot she finds that a 5:30 A.M. train bringing supplies to the restaurant has just left. Now she must chase the train and try to intercept it. She finally does; help comes and the problems are solved.

The epilogue takes place at a performance of the Spanish Riding School in Vienna and a welcoming home of the stolen horse, which also takes part in the performance. Tradition has indicated, one learns, that the name of the missing horse will still be above its stall and fresh straw will be waiting.

Airs above the Ground derives its title from the steps and the formations, the jumps and lifts, that the best of the Lipizzan Stallions perform after years of training. Vanessa is the one who discovers that the recovering piebald is a former Lipizzan when she takes him to graze on the hillside nearby while the circus is going on. Suddenly, during the waltz music from *The Rosenkavalier,* the piebald begins the movements and then the first of the difficult "airs above the ground" that it had learned years before.

As in most of Stewart's suspense novels, characterization is secondary to plot, yet the characters of Vanessa and Timothy are well drawn. Lewis remains in the background until close to the end. Vanessa is strong in the same way that the other Stewart heroines are strong. She is independent, courageous, and ingenious in getting out of difficult situations and in making decisions under pressure. This is the only novel in which the main character is married, but Vanessa and Lewis are separated during most of the action. When they are together even in difficult circumstances, as when they are stalking Sandor, they have a playful camaraderie, a bantering exchange of humor, as the characters in a James Bond movie might have.

Timothy functions as Vanessa's partner or younger brother. He is eager to experience life on his own and is protective toward her but entirely helpless when he injures his leg and is in the shadow of death, so to speak. Lewis is the mysterious male hovering in the background, as seen in several of the Stewart stories, wholly confident and capable of overcoming the villain.

Humor emerges at unforeseen moments, such as during the major battle involving the Beckers, Sandor Balog, Lewis, Vanessa, and Timothy. Frau Becker—a huge woman, poker in hand, undaunted by the gun Vanessa holds, and dismayed only by the sight of her broken china—charges at Lewis. Vanessa tries to intercept, with little success: "It was all I could do not to shoot her myself. For two or three sizzling minutes all I could hope for was to hold on madly to the hand which held the poker, and prevent my own gun from going off, as I was shaken about that room like a terrier hanging on to a maddened cow."[3]

For this novel Mary Stewart has had a field day with the chapter headings. In *This Rough Magic* all quotations came from *The Tempest*; here the selections for the twenty-one chapters plus epilogue come from a variety of sources, including seven different Shakespearean plays, in addition to his poem *Venus and Adonis,* and quotations from Christopher Marlowe, Robert Browning, John Keats, Robert Burns, and such unlikely candidates as Mark Twain, W. S. Gilbert, and Artemus Ward. The effect is titillating and gives the whole work a light touch. No matter how serious or violent the action within, the chapter headings remind the reader that the book is, nevertheless, a clever, witty, well-planned entertainment.

A good example is chapter 14, in which Sandor Balog appears in Vanessa's room, demanding the saddle. He not only threatens but hits her and forces her to dress to go with him so that she will not call the police or alarm the others. When he steps to the door to check the corridor, she slips through the side door leading to battlements (roof), and the breathtaking chase begins. The particular quotation heading this chapter is from Artemus Ward's "A Visit to Brigham Young." Ward says, in his inimitable style of misspellings, "I girdid up my Lions & fled the Seen."[4]

The Gabriel Hounds

Mary Stewart's careful plotting, her talent for creating suspense, her ability to immerse the reader in specific surroundings, planned for by much detail, and her knowledge of psychology and motivation, in addition to skillful writing, make her work highly readable and believable despite seemingly bizarre circumstances, all of which the reader finds in *The Gabriel Hounds* (1965). Of Stewart's suspense novels, this one most closely fits the pattern of the gothic with a touch of decaying Arabian nights; part of the unusual atmosphere stems from its location, in Lebanon, and the fact that there is an old, semideserted, crumbling palace, about thirty miles from Beirut, set in a mountainous, rocky, sparsely populated region.

The inspiration for the plot came partly from visits to the area but mainly from the real-life story of Lady Hester Stanhope (1776–1839), the eldest daughter of Charles, Viscount Mahon (afterward third Earl of Stanhope), by his first wife, sister of William Pitt. Lady Hester Stanhope possessed a brilliant and dynamic personality, but eventually, impatient with the restrictions of ordinary society, she left England (in 1810) for the Mideast with a Welsh companion, an English physician, and others. After a shipwreck off Rhodes, she traveled to Jerusalem, crossed the desert, and finally settled down among the natives on the slopes of Mount Lebanon. There she built a group of houses surrounded by a garden and an outer wall, like a medieval fortress. In the following years she acquired several slaves and exerted much local and political power. She entertained important European personages visiting in the area and adopted Mideastern manners, customs, and dress. She also maintained numerous cats and other animals. Later, accumulating large debts with her extravagant life-style, she became increasingly eccentric and bitter, finally, in the last year of her life, shutting herself up in her stronghold with five servants, walling up the gate, and refusing to see any more visitors. Hearing that she was ill, the British consul at Beirut and a missionary rode over the mountains to see her but arrived just after her death. They found the place deserted, for all the servants had fled and taken with them everything movable. The consul and the missionary performed the final rites by burying Lady Stanhope in the garden at midnight.

The character in the novel patterned on Lady Stanhope is Harriet Boyd, an elderly, autocratic woman who has lived in the Mideast most of her life, with only periodic visits back to England. She has renounced her English citizenship and given several notices to English relatives that they are virtually cut out of her will.

The protagonist, Christy (Christabel) Mansel, is visiting Damascus and Beirut with a tour but has just left the group. In Damascus she meets her cousin Charles, whom she hasn't seen in four years, when her branch of the family moved from England to Los Angeles. Charles persuades Christy to go with him to visit Great-Aunt Harriet living near Beirut. Christy has not seen Great-Aunt Harriet for fifteen years, but because Charles cannot join her immediately, she, with spare time, decides to go ahead by herself and pave the way.

Christy hires a car and a driver for the trip into the mountains.
Excellent description follows of the countryside they pass and of a little
village in which they stop to buy oranges. Christy is much aware of
the legends surrounding this region of the Adonis River. Egyptian,
Greek, and Christian myths, she knows, are part of this heritage, but
she likes most the well-known story of Aphrodite, who fell in love
with the Syrian shepherd Adonis, lying with him among the flowers.
Here the wild boar killed Adonis, and flowers (anemones) grew wher-
ever his blood splashed; as a result, so legend goes, every spring the
waters of the Adonis River still flow red as they reach down to the sea.
Christy, like most of Mary Stewart's main characters, is inquisitive,
intelligent, and well educated.

Christy's driver, Hamid, then shows her in the distance the big ram-
bling palace Dar Ibrahim, well known in the area, belonging to her
great-aunt. It is unaccessible from the road and must be reached by a
rocky path down to a stream and then up the mountain.

Hamid accompanies Christy, but they have trouble getting in, since
the old Arab gatekeeper has orders to keep everyone out. When they
do enter, she is shocked to see the condition of the place: "The whole
place had the air of something deserted long since, and lived in only
by rats and mice and spiders. Not a floor but was filthy, with gaps in
the ornamental tiling; the wall mosaics were dim and battered, the
window grilles broken, the lintels cracked. A heavy, dusty silence slept
over everything like a grey blanket. . . . It was a far cry from the
'enchanted palace' that imagination—more powerful than reason—had
led me to expect."[5]

All the elements for the typical gothic story are present, complete
with secret passageways and subterranean rooms, fierce dogs and mysterious inhabitants. John Lethman, Great-Aunt Harriet's doctor, they
are led to believe, comes to meet them, but he explains that he is
simply doing research and writing and has been living here for almost
a year. He tells Christy that she cannot see her great-aunt now, for the
woman is sleeping; she must see her at night. Although Lethman is
reluctant to do so, he says Christy may stay and the driver Hamid is
to fetch her down at the road the next morning.

The enclosed grounds include several buildings, gardens, and a
small lake with an island. The section of the palace where Christy is
to stay is the Seraglio, in years past the harem quarters with barred
windows.

With growing apprehension, Christy is ushered that night into the bedroom of Great-Aunt Harriet. This meeting takes place in chapter 5, at the beginning of which is a quotation from Coleridge's poem "Christabel":

> There came
> A tongue of light, a fit of flame;
> And Christabel saw the lady's eye,
> And nothing else saw she thereby.[6]

Such is the case; she sees little. In the dimly lit room in the shadows of the bed curtains sits, like a Buddha, the person that to Christy seems a fantastically robed Eastern male. She speaks in an asthmatic, husky voice and wears a turban that, when it becomes a bit dislodged, shows a shaved head. To Christy, the only recognizable feature is the huge ruby ring, famous in the family, the gift of a Baghdad prince. As Christy chats about the family, she wonders why the elderly woman has not mentioned Charles, her favorite relative, and when Christy asks if Charles can come to visit, the great-aunt says no.

The concentration of the novel is on the mystery of Great-Aunt Harriet, and one is reminded that her life-style purposely follows somewhat that of Lady Hester Stanhope, a person she much admired. But the bizarre interview with Christy alerts the reader that all is not well, and from there on, events move quickly.

A heavy rainstorm that night floods the stream so that when Christy goes the next morning to meet Hamid, she cannot cross. Charles, however, has come instead, and they both climb to higher ground upstream, searching for a place for him to cross over. After a conference with Christy, Charles is increasingly concerned about Great-Aunt Harriet; he is afraid she may be the victim of foul play. The plan then is that Christy is to go back and ask to spend another night, while Charles sneaks in at a designated open window if she cannot locate the proper door to the back entrance; from their present position high above the back of the palace they have seen someone entering there.

Back within the grounds, Christy spends several hours in a futile search for the door leading to the apparently secret stairway and back entrance. As to approachable entrances, she finds only one partly shuttered window, which late that night she manages to pry open. In the dark, the dangerous dogs—two large Persian greyhounds—appear, but Christy finds that despite warnings they are not dangerous. The reader experiences anxious, suspenseful moments during Christy's searches and subsequent unexpected meeting with John Lethman.

Later Charles climbs in, and the two search for the hidden door and underground passageway. In the process, they also find in underground rooms supplies of mysterious tin boxes. Great-Aunt Harriet's room is empty. Charles leaves Christy and says he will meet her in Beirut the next morning.

Charles never appears in Beirut, but a letter informs Christy that he has gone on to Damascus to meet a friend. When she tries to follow him, she is stopped at the border for lack of the proper visa. On her way back to Beirut, she is kidnapped and brought back to Dar Ibrahim.

One discovers now that both Charles and she are captives. From chapter 14 through chapter 18 are much excitement and several revelations. One finds that Great-Aunt Harriet has died two weeks before of a heart attack, complicated by gastric attacks from doses of a purgative oil given her by Halide, an attractive native woman having an affair with John Lethman. Christy has seen Halide wearing Harriet's ruby ring.

Harriet's former physician, Dr. Henry Grafton, is involved in drug trafficking and has impersonated the old lady for Christy's visit; he and John Lethman have been using the palace for a lucrative cocaine and opium-smuggling business. The unexpected death of the old lady has complicated their work, and they did not report her death; in fact, when Dr. Grafton discovers that Halide is responsible, in anger he strikes and inadvertently kills her.

A final violent showdown between Christy and Dr. Grafton leads to a chain of events that includes a skirmish between the dogs and the cat, an overturned lamp, spilled oil, and a fire. Once the fire starts, it spreads rapidly. At one point Christy, with the dogs, takes refuge on the little island in the lake. So do all the animals (including the rats) on the premises. Christy is rescued by Charles, who earlier escaped, and they leave by the underground passage (for which he now has the key) to the higher ground behind the palace.

When they are free at last, they see the native village people gathering at the front gates. They also see Lethman escape on horseback and Dr. Grafton shot by Halide's brother as the doctor gathers part of the valuable packages to take with him.

There has been a first declaration of love between Christy and Charles on the island during the fire as they prepare to leave with the dogs to flee to safety; one assumes they intend to live happily ever after once their lives return to normal.

Christy's English family is wealthy, and she is several times referred to as a "spoiled bitch" by Grafton and Lethman when she shows spirit and courage in dealing with them. She refuses to be intimidated; otherwise, she is the same bright, positive, resourceful woman as Stewart's other protagonists. She and Charles carry on the same good-natured banter as do the young couples in Stewart's other suspense novels. Charles, too, is brave, resourceful, witty, and a match for any villain.

The principal villain is Dr. Henry Grafton, a Turkish citizen who has been carrying on the illegal trade for some time. One is led to believe, however, that he has been conscientious in looking after Great-Aunt Harriet's health. The secluded palace is ideal for his illegal business. John Lethman, actually an archaeologist, is a more sympathetic character, for he has become a victim, being both lured into the enterprise and lured into becoming an addict.

Besides Dr. Grafton, Halide is the other essentially villainous character. She shows envy and hate for Christy, viewing her as a rival for the affections of John Lethman. Halide has (when the doctor was not at hand) put the poisonous oil in Great-Aunt Harriet's food to make her ill and more tractable, nursing her afterward and receiving awards for doing so. Halide would gladly eliminate Christy if she dared and does put the dangerous purgative in Christy's soup, which Christy luckily does not eat.

The title of the novel comes from an English north country tale; the Gabriel Hounds are a pack of dogs that run with death, and when someone is going to die, one hears the dogs howling at night. Another reason for the title is that Great-Aunt Harriet had a pair of valuable (Ming) china dogs that Charles had admired since boyhood and called the Gabriel Hounds because they resembled the illustrations of the dogs in his book. He sees the china dogs again neglected and dusty in an underground storage room with other objects, but presumably they are destroyed in the fire. Earlier, several times during the course of the story a summons—Christy assumes from Great-Aunt Harriet—results in the loud clanging of a bell, followed immediately by the howling of the hounds.

Charles and Christy have been brought up almost like brother and sister, and their fathers are identical twins; therefore they are in a sense closer than most first cousins, a situation that apparently does not disturb them. But why, one wonders, did Mary Stewart choose to create

and then not use for a specific purpose this slightly incestuous relationship? That is a mystery left unsolved.

Touch Not the Cat

Nine years elapsed between the publication of *Touch Not the Cat*
(1976) and the previous suspense novel; this story marks a straying
from the pattern with a more involved narrative technique than in the
other works of suspense, the result of the interweaving of two separate
but related stories and added impressionism.

In addition to being set in England, *Touch Not the Cat* resembles *The
Ivy Tree* in several ways. The leading characters are not outsiders coming for a vacation; this land is home territory, the place in which they
grew up. The mysteries and the problems are an essential part of their
own lives, involving their identities, family relationships, and questions regarding the future. In both novels more emphasis is placed on
characterization; plot is still intricate and all-important, but the working out of the plots involves the lives and love relationships of the
protagonists.

In both novels the home is the center; the estates carry tradition. In
Touch Not the Cat, Ashley Court is of historic significance, complete
with moat and maze, stemming, with variations, from Saxon times; it
has, however, become an albatross, for recent family owners have not
had sufficient funds to keep it from falling into decay. Even though
the house is open to the public, there is not the money needed for
upkeep—to trim the hedges, to tend the gardens, or to make the necessary repairs to the main house and outlying buildings. Already most
of the family silver and valuable art objects have been sold.

The female narrator is telling the story one year after the events have
taken place, and the account begins with a lighthearted history of the
Ashley family from Saxon times. With humor she explains that the
Ashley family members have always been opportunists and extremely
flexible, retaining what they wished and adapting "without effort to
the winning side." She says in part: "We were Catholics right up to
Henry VIII. Then when the Great Whore got him we built a priest's
hole and kept it tenanted until we saw which side the wafer was but-
tered, and then somehow there we were under Elizabeth, staunch Prot-
estants and bricking up the priest's hole, and learning the Thirty-nine
Articles off by heart probably aloud."[7]

Bryony Ashley, the central character and narrator, also explains about the unusual gift she has, one that has been prevalent in varying degrees in the family since Elizabeth Ashley was burned at the stake in 1623. Bryony has the ability to communicate by thought transference with a particular member of the family and has done so for years, yet she doesn't know who that other person is. She has by this time (she is now twenty-one) come to think of him as "lover." Apparently the other partner has been as unwilling as she to talk about this relationship; the difference is that he knows who she is and calls her by name but indicates that it is not time to reveal himself. The identity of this person is one of the mysteries to be solved during the course of the story.

The actual sequence of events begins in Funchal, on the island of Madeira, where Bryony is working temporarily as a receptionist and tour guide. She has been away from home in England for about eight months, having originally accompanied her father to a sanitorium in Germany to recover his health. After one month's stay there and his continued improvement, she has taken the job in sunny Madeira rather than return to England for the winter.

One night as she awakens with feelings of dread, she receives a telepathic message from her "lover" that something is wrong and she should go to her father; almost immediately she receives a telephone call confirming the message. These events occur in chapter 1.

At the beginning of the next chapter Bryony is already on her way to the sanitorium at Bad Tolz, for it was Dr. Walther Gothard calling to say that her father had been injured in a hit-and-run accident; unfortunately, Jonathan Ashley is already dead when she arrives. The police are investigating, and one of them has recorded the disjointed, incoherent sentences of Jonathan's last words to his daughter. Part of the message warns her of danger, but the rest no one else can decipher. The details of this message, naturally, are parts of the puzzle to be solved in the remainder of the book. Another question is the identity of the hit-and-run driver.

Jonathan Ashley's body is cremated after which Bryony comes home to Ashley Court and the cottage in which she and her father lived. By tradition and the family trust, the estate goes to the nearest male relative, Howard Ashley, a cousin of her father's living in Spain. Howard's sons, Francis, Emory, and James, have been Bryony's childhood playmates. Emory and James are identical twins and even at twenty-seven are still too much alike to be separately identified by most people; Bryony is one of the few who can distinguish between them. The

sons—except for Francis the poet, who is off traveling somewhere—
have been working in their father's business in Bristol and in Spain.
The biggest mystery involves the twins and their strange behavior. As
they have always done, Emory and James substitute for each other
when alibis are needed or when it suits them to do so.

Emory has become involved with Cathy Underhill, the daughter of
a wealthy American family currently renting a part of the big house.
Missing valuable objects from the house add to the problems.

One discovers that neither Emory nor James wants Ashley Court,
since their father is in poor health and their own business is in financial
distress, but they do want the money that the sale of the estate would
bring. Before they are legally entitled to do so, they secretly sell several
valuable objects from the house. The Underhills, upset when they learn
that their daughter Cathy has been helping the twins acquire these
objects, decide to sever the connection between Cathy and Emory and
move to London.

One of the causes of friction is that Bryony is the owner of the
cottage in which she has been living and that includes the strip of land
necessary as an access to the main road. Without this, no one can easily
sell the property.

Bryony has resumed her friendship with Rob Granger, the young
man—also a childhood companion—whom the others consider only
the "farmer's son," a caretaker of the estate, living also in one of its
cottages.

Bryony has thought for some time that her cousin James might be
the silent "lover," a belief that creates suspense especially when she
suspects with some evidence that he and Emory may have been responsible for her father's death; furthermore, she has reason to fear harm
from them. Even so, late one night in an emotional moment, she
knows, from an insistent telepathic message, that the "lover" she seeks
is waiting for her outside in the garden, and she runs out. The tension
is great, for the reader suspects that the "lover" may be waiting to
harm her.

But standing there under the pear tree is Rob Granger, watching
the house to see that Bryony is safe. As she comes to him, he admits
that he is her secret friend; he has not identified himself before because
he knew she was infatuated with James and feared she might be disappointed. On the contrary, she is elated, and both are caught up in
the joy of the moment. Rob then suggests the wild idea of being mar-

ried the next day by the vicar on the estate; actually, he confesses, he has had the license for two weeks. Bryony agrees. Rob has the Ashley gift of thought transference because he is indeed an Ashley through the secret marriage (although he does not know it at this time) of Nicholas Ashley, his great-grandfather, and Ellen Makepeace, a local woman.

The impromptu wedding of Bryony and Rob takes place the next morning, and that evening as Bryony waits for Rob to return, with a storm threatening, she receives a surprise visit from Emory and James. Not expecting her to be there, they have apparently opened the sluice that will allow the river to overflow the waters in the moat and thereby inundate the cottage and the lower grounds. This was to be their way of encouraging Bryony to leave and sell them the property, which in the past she has not been inclined to do.

During this critical time in which the twins have become increasingly menacing, the bookseller from the village calls to report that the book Bryony has sent him from the library collection and mentioned in her father's last message is indeed from the sixteenth century (one of only four) and extremely valuable; moreover, fastened under the bookmark in the front is the missing page from the parish register and a note certifying the marriage of Nicholas Ashley and Ellen Makepeace. In other words, Rob, the twins realize, is a legitimate heir to the estate. Although Bryony protests that neither she nor Rob has plans to stay, for they wish to immigrate to New Zealand—a dream Rob has had for some time—Emory fears that the court entanglements might take years. In anger when he realizes that Bryony may by telepathy call Rob for help, Emory hits her over the head.

She wakes to find herself in the space under the pavilion floor with no apparent escape. The waters are rising and beginning to flood the area. She knows too that the twins will try to waylay and attack Rob when he comes to her aid; nevertheless, all turns out well when Emory becomes injured and entangled in the stream and James tries to rescue him. In the nick of time as the waters are rising, Bryony is able to loosen planking from the decayed floor and safely lets herself up to the ground floor of the pavilion.

When the crisis is over and the twins have fled, the third brother, the gentle cousin Francis, arrives. Bryony and Rob tell him the whole story and also that the sale of the valuable book would not only cover his family's debt but also endow the property so that it can become a trust and thus affordable. As far as Bryony and Rob are concerned,

Francis is welcome to Ashley Court, which he loves, and they will move to New Zealand, where Rob's great-grandmother and her brothers moved so hastily many years before.

As to the interweaving of the separate but related stories, near the end of chapter 1 and at the end of every chapter throughout the book appear short sections of the tale, told in the third person, of Nicholas, the great-grandfather—from the first impatient waiting in the pavilion for his secret love, Ellen Makepeace, to their love tryst, and finally, as he leaves the pavilion and maze, to his death at the hands of Ellen's brothers. One has learned earlier in the regular narrative that the wild, headstrong Nicholas had been shot; as the vignettes dated 1835 progress, the reader is exposed to the impressionistic portions of the final story as seen through Nicholas's eyes. Not until the end of chapter 4, however, does the reader know who this person is. Because of the more intricate narrative technique and the thought-transference passages, this novel requires more careful reader attention and concentration than Stewart's other suspense tales.

As to characterization, Bryony is a typical Stewart heroine, although more vulnerable and emotionally involved in the events that affect her life and her future. The novel contains less verbal game playing, and the male-female encounters are more serious. Rob Granger, the "farm boy," may not be as verbally adroit as some of the other Stewart heroes, but he has all of their good qualities, including intelligence. He is earthy but has an innate gentility. He has loved Bryony for a long time but has recognized the difference in their situations, even though Bryony and her father have been poor for many years. Rob is self-assured, possessing a different kind of confidence than that of the twins.

Emory and James are confident in their ability to charm and manipulate others. Emory is the older twin, more ruthless, and the leader in their escapades. He is also the one responsible for Bryony's father's death, but that, apparently, was not intentional. James goes along with all his brother does and defends him right or wrong. Bryony is shocked, however, to discover the extent of the twins' criminal mentality.

The book's title refers to "Touch Not the Cat but the Glove," the present family motto adopted by William Ashley, father of Nicholas, to honor his lovely young wife, whose family motto it was. The cat was a Scottish wildcat, and it was William Ashley in the 1820s who shaped the maze in the pattern of the family crest and built the pavilion in the center.

"Touch Me Who Dares" was the original Ashley motto, meaning essentially the same, and the leopard was the animal on the crest, having been suggested from the mosaic Roman leopard that Bryony discovers after the flood on the underfloor surface of the pavilion. This had been the site of a Roman house.

All the chapter headings in this novel come from *Romeo and Juliet*. The quotations are appropriate since William Ashley had written for his wife a book of poems entitled *The New Romeo* and the very valuable book (so important in the plot) was the pre-Shakespearean, 1562 edition of *The Tragicall History of Romeus and Juliet*, a long poem by Arthur Brooke. Bryony refers to Rob Granger and herself as "star-crossed lovers." When trapped and seeing the rising waters, she considers how people will view their deaths with no inkling of blame for the twins: "The two of us, star-crossed lovers, drowned on our wedding night as the flood swept through the cottage; and all the while the twins, securely alibied, miles away." (*TNC*, 255).

As it happens, however, after Rob fights his way through the maze and to the pavilion and the danger is over, they end up, wet, dirty, and exhausted, spending their wedding night in the pavilion, the favorite trysting place of their ancestor Nicholas Ashley.

Chapter Five
The Arthurian Novels: Merlin

The Crystal Cave

The move from the suspense novel to the Arthurian legend was a gigantic step forward, not because Stewart's suspense tales are lesser works but because the novels of Merlin, Arthur, and Mordred try to do much more and succeed amazingly well. Stewart, in these works, employs no plot patterns as she does in the earlier novels.

The narrative technique is straightforward. Events are treated chronologically, although they are presented in the first three books as Merlin's memories when he is already old and, as he admits, when most of his supernatural powers are gone. Characterization becomes much more important and the suspense techniques more subtle in these later works. The pace is more leisurely as the stories unfold in sequence so that by the end of the fourth, *The Wicked Day* (1983), all the principal characters are gone: Merlin in retirement, Mordred and Arthur dead, and Guinevere in a nunnery.

The Arthurian legends are as powerful today as they were centuries ago. The Camelot tale and the differing versions of Arthur and Guinevere, as well as Arthur and the Knights of the Round Table, continue to be popular story and theater material. Previous writers have sought as their sources Sir Thomas Malory's *Morte d'Arthur,* printed in 1485, and the works of the twelfth-century Chretien de Troyes, who inspired the French romances and the legendary conception of the lives and loves of these heroic characters. In later times the most popular version (also from these sources) was Alfred Tennyson's *Idylls of the King* (1859).

Since the mid-twentieth century, there has been a proliferation of literary works about the Arthurian world. Many of these took the form of fantasy and science fiction; others were modern versions of the Arthurian legends. A fairly recent trend, however, has been toward a more historical treatment of fifth- and sixth-century Britain. As Geoffrey Ashe, well-known Arthurian scholar, states in *The Quest for Arthur's Britain,* "Solid facts began to emerge into daylight through the labours of archaeologists."[1] These findings and the work of such historians as

John Morris and Leslie Alcock have encouraged authors to consider the legendary figures as real people and to write about them as such. These novelists, often medieval specialists, are stripping away the fantastic elements and are creating people who might have lived in this mysterious world of post-Roman Britain; the resultant creations, though well researched and seemingly authentic, vary greatly from writer to writer. There are not enough available facts to achieve consistency.

Guinevere, for instance, in some versions has a Christian upbringing; in others, a pagan one. Her infidelities with Lancelot, who is seldom given that name, are depicted in varying degrees of innocence. And Godfrey Turton's Merlin in *The Emperor Arthur* (1967) is a Druid priest who conspires with the Saxons behind Arthur's back—a far cry from Mary Stewart's conceptions of Merlin in these novels.

These were confusing, turbulent times, with pagan religions observed side by side, though often hidden with the Christian one. In history, the actual years of this short period of Arthurian influence and the time span of the four Stewart novels is about a hundred years, from shortly after the Roman withdrawal from Britain (the story begins around 445) to the supposed years of Arthur's death, around 537 or 539. Politically, they were years of unrest for the Celtic nation, as the several minor kings throughout Britain tried to maintain control of and stability for their lands and people. The major danger came from the waves of invading Saxons who had already gained a foothold in southeastern Britain, but the most immediate problems stemmed from power struggles for leadership. The years of Arthur's supposed reign were thought to be relatively calm and stable, but after his death the Saxons, along with the Angles and the Jutes, soon established dominance over the island of Britain. Throughout the four novels are periodic battles against not only the Saxon invaders but also the Picts from the north, the Angles from the east, and the Irish from the west.

Taylor and Brewer, in their discussion of Arthurian works, call *The Crystal Cave* (1970) one of the most successful Romano-British Arthurian romances,[2] and Geoffrey Ashe cites Mary Stewart as one of the "distinguished names in this field"[3] of writers, experts in the period. Mary Stewart, however, acknowledges that she is primarily a storyteller and not a historian. Among problems in dealing with this material was the need to make compromises with place names so that readers would not be hopelessly confused or need to spend an inordinate amount of time studying glossaries. Stewart has also had to invent characters and circumstances to explain events and has taken as her primary source

The History of the Kings of Britain, by the monk Geoffrey of Monmouth (1136), who, historians agree, although he gained material from Welsh poetry, folktales, and legends and the writers Gildas and Nennius, invented much also. Most of these later historic writers have relied on Geoffrey as their primary source.

Stewart has maintained that her poet's ear in regard to names and the character of speech was the final determinant in the material she chose. What sounded right to her, she felt, would also be appropriate and right for her readers. Geoffrey of Monmouth may not have been an accurate historian, but he had, she maintains, a good story to tell. Her Merlin is a combination of four people: prince, prophet, poet, and engineer. In *The Crystal Cave* his early training, the varied, extensive education and the lessons learned as a necessity for survival, in addition to the supernatural gifts he possessed (the "sight"), guided and sharpened by a wise old man also gifted with prophetic powers, made him superior to the ordinary man.

The Plot

The story begins in Maridunum in South Wales, as Merlin, the narrator, looking back over the years, is six years old. Already his life has been difficult, for he has been born a bastard; his unmarried mother, the king's daughter, has also refused information about who the boy's father is. Merlin's grandfather does not want the boy in his presence; therefore, Merlin has none of the privileges or respect of a young prince. Except for irritating confrontations with a more robust and aggressive cousin Dinias, Merlin finds himself most often alone, and he delights in playing in the unused heating ducts under the palace (a former Roman building), where he also overhears conversations among the grown-ups; thus, early in life he learns more than he sometimes understands. The king would like his daughter, Merlin's mother, to marry one of the princes of Britain or Brittany, but she refuses to accept a husband. She has become a Christian, and she prefers, she says, to enter the nearby nunnery of St. Peter.

Just after Merlin has suffered the public humiliation of having been struck by his grandfather, his Uncle Camlach, lately returned to the town of Maridunum, tries to poison the boy. This incident is one of the first in which Merlin's "sight" tells him that the apricot handed him by Camlach is poisoned.

Camlach then wants Merlin to train to become a priest so that he will never be a rival for the kingship; thereafter Merlin begins more serious studies with a tutor, Demetrius, a Greek slave who has a "genius for languages." Merlin still seeks time alone, and one day, riding into the hills, he comes upon a cave belonging to Galapas, the wise old mystic. Galapas teaches Merlin many secrets of nature, including the healing properties of plants, and then in the deepest recesses of the cave, lined with crystals that reflect the light, he lets Merlin experience the first of his visions, scenes of future or sometimes present but faraway events.

By this time Merlin is twelve years old, and on an important trip he accompanies the king and the rest of the adult male household for a meeting with the High King Vortigern in the north of Wales at Segontium. Vortigern is beset with anxieties of not only increasing Saxon pressures but threat of invasion from Brittany by the sons of the king whose throne he usurped and their brother, whom Vortigern has had murdered. His own sons are also in revolt.

Several months later in the Crystal Cave, Merlin sees a vision of his grandfather's accidental death, caused by falling when a slave, Merlin's own servant Cerdic, spills oil from a lamp. As Merlin rides home, he finds that these events have indeed occurred and with horror he discovers Cerdic in his room with his throat cut. Merlin knows that his own life is now in danger; therefore, as a burial rite for Cerdic, he sets fire to his room and flees from the palace. But outside in the dark, as Merlin leaps over the wall, he is kidnapped by two strange men who take him aboard a ship sailing on a four-day journey to Lesser Britain (Brittany).

Once the ship has anchored, Merlin manages to escape. He has no money or warm clothes and, afraid of being caught, hides outside the walled town in the horse stable of a nearby encampment. In the midst of a vision as he leaves the stable, Merlin is found by Ambrosius and his brother Uther. Ambrosius is the military leader of the army being readied for an attack on Vortigern in Britain; it was his and Uther's brother whom Vortigern had killed, and for years they have prepared to regain their rightful leadership and the kingship. Ambrosius takes Merlin into his protection, and then one becomes aware that Ambrosius is Merlin's real father. Merlin's mother has never revealed the truth about the secret love affair with the wounded enemy prince whom she discovered and hid in the Crystal Cave until he was well. He was eighteen and she was younger. Ambrosius and Uther, though Celts, have become Romanized with a military operation that is efficient and powerful.

Merlin now gains a tutor who specializes in mathematics and astronomy; also from others he learns engineering skills. He discovers, too, some of the secrets of the Druids, of which his tutor Belasius is an archpriest. Ambrosius, Uther, and most of their soldiers are followers of the Roman-adopted Persian god Mithras. Young as he is, Merlin becomes the subject of awe. The men see him now as the prince he is but are also increasingly aware of his unusual powers.

The years pass, and in the spring of his eighteenth year Merlin makes a secret trip back to Britain to his former home in Maridunum. He hopes to visit his mother at the convent and, for Ambrosius, find out what he can about Vortigern's movements. The armies are ready to invade Britain. His uncle Camlach, who earlier sided with the rebellious sons of Vortigern, is now dead; the former palace of his grandfather is deserted, except for sustaining his cousin Dinias, living by himself in a threadbare existence; and when Merlin visits the Crystal Cave, he finds it empty and Galapas dead.

Later, Merlin is apprehended by Vortigern's men, who take Merlin, along with his mother, before the High King to the location where Vortigern has been trying unsuccessfully to build an impregnable fortress. As the walls are built up each day, they collapse by night; Vortigern's priests have told him that a sacrifice is required to appease the gods. The victim must be someone not of regular birth, someone not human. When Merlin's mother, not knowing why they have been called before the king, repeats the fabricated tale that the boy's father was a mysterious figure who had appeared only in dreams, materializing by night, the king declares Merlin born of the prince of darkness and thus appropriate for the sacrifice needed. The king is not aware of the connection between Merlin and Ambrosius, but Merlin fears that he may be. Taking the initiative and remembering the area from his Segontium visit years before and the cave leading to an underground pool, Merlin immediately tells the king that he can show him why the walls of the fortress will not stand; thereupon, he directs the king and his men to drain this pool. They do so, and when Merlin makes prophecies that indicate Vortigern's defeat by outside forces, Vortigern and his men leave the area and prepare elsewhere for the coming invasions.

Ambrosius and Uther and their armies do invade and rally other groups against Vortigern. These battles lead to the death of Vortigern and the crowning of Ambrosius. Saxon elements continue to be a problem. Merlin has become even more a subject of awe, as the soldiers believe his presence brings victory and as he performs the seemingly impossible task of bringing from Ireland the central sacred Standing Stone, which, in an engineering feat, he joins to the other ancient standing stones in the Stonehenge area, principally, it turns out, as a memorial for Ambrosius. Ambrosius is an excellent leader, but he dies within two years and his brother Uther, less qualified, becomes king. Uther has always been wary of Merlin and therefore agrees to Merlin's request to go back to the Crystal Cave area to live with his servant Cadal; however, at his coronation Uther sends for Merlin so that with his extraordinary powers Merlin may help him gain the love and possession of Ygraine, young wife of Gorlois, the elderly Duke of Cornwall.

Once this task has been initiated, Merlin's prophetic vision allows him to foresee that the child of this union will be a great king. Everything in his life, Merlin feels, is leading up to the coming (as the reader is aware) of King Arthur. With Ygraine's permission Merlin arranges a secret meeting with Uther and their disguised group to go to Tintagel, the castle fortress on the coast of Cornwall, home of Ygraine, while Gorlois, unsuspecting, is waiting elsewhere to do battle with the king's forces.

Ironically, the same night as Arthur is conceived, the duke is killed in battle, paving the way for Uther's eventual marriage to Ygraine. When word of the duke's death is brought unexpectedly to the castle by two of his trusted men, there is bloodshed. Merlin himself is forced into a life-and-death struggle with Brithnael, a loyal supporter of the duke; as Uther leaves Tintagel, however, instead of being grateful to Merlin for his aid, he is furious with Merlin for not having foreseen the duke's death. Furthermore, if there is a bastard child conceived from that evening, he says, he will have nothing to do with it, and he warns Merlin to get out of his life and to stay away from him.

As the novel ends, Merlin, still at Tintagel that night and himself wounded, mourns the death of Cadal. Ironically, he receives no thanks for help given but finds himself again an outsider, as he was in the early years. His life has come full circle, but in the stars he sees hope in the coming birth of the young child. Before Cadal dies, Merlin tells him the prophecy that ends the novel on a positive note: Ygraine will

send the child to Merlin, who will take him out of the king's reach
and keep him safe, passing on to him his knowledge, and when the
boy is grown he will come back and be crowned king.

Structure

In addition to containing a prologue, the novel is divided into five
books. In the prologue, entitled "The Prince of Darkness," Merlin introduces himself and presents the vision he has had of the farewell
encounter of the eighteen-year-old mysterious prince and the young
princess at the Crystal Cave: his father and mother.

Each of the five sections of the book is given the name of a bird or
an animal representative of either Merlin or an important figure in his
life. Merlin's full Welsh name is Myrddin Emrys, but he is called Merlin, meaning "falcon." In Book I, entitled "The Dove," the young boy
is not yet the full-grown falcon, and in his precarious existence he is
like the ringdove that survives by being quiet and running away when
danger appears. The dove becomes "The Falcon" of Book II when he is
twelve years old and arrives, kidnapped and on his own, in the strange
territory of Brittany (called Less Britain); at the end of Book II he has
become the established son of Ambrosius. Book III, opening five years
later, is entitled, "The Wolf," the designation for the enemy king Vortigern, the crafty leader hoping to sacrifice Merlin for the sake of his
fortress; when Merlin persuades Vortigern to drain the pool, he prophesies that there will be a white dragon and a red dragon at the bot-
tom. Symbolically, this becomes true when Vortigern's white-dragon
banner falls into the shallow water of the pool, whereupon Merlin directs the attention of Vortigern and the bystanders skyward to a fiery
comet, or dragon of fire, and calls upon Vortigern to strike his tents
and leave, for, he says, the red dragon has come, and Vortigern is
convinced that this is so. Book IV, entitled, "The Red Dragon"—the
symbol of Ambrosius and Uther Pendragon—deals with the successful
invasion of Britain and Ambrosius's kingship until his death. Book V,
"The Coming of the Bear," involves the coming together of Uther, now
king, and Ygraine, as well as the heralding of Arthur, symbolized as
the bear, Artos meaning "bear" in Celtic.

Suspense is sustained throughout the novel in the conflicts Merlin
undergoes. For him, life is uncertain, and he finds himself in a series
of dangerous situations. He must struggle first to survive and then to
overcome the prejudices and resentments of others against him. He

must also come to grips with his strange powers. Much is expected of him, but he is often misunderstood; he becomes a doctor, an engineer, and a prophet as needed. Later, people are afraid of him and of what they do not understand. He is sometimes accused of being cold and unfeeling; even though that is not the case, his is a lonely existence.

There are many ironies throughout. One of the greatest, as mentioned previously, comes at the end of the novel when Uther accuses Merlin of being self-serving and ambitious. He says: "I tell you, Merlin, you shall not use me. I'll no longer be a puppet for you to pull the strings. So keep away from me."[4] The truth is that it is Merlin who is "used" by those anxious to gain their own ends.

Characterization

Merlin is intensely human and sympathetic, first as a child and then as a young man struggling against the unfortunate circumstances surrounding him. He is neither overly strong nor a good rider, and he gets sick on sea journeys. He remains the underdog until Ambrosius declares him his son, and at the end he is alone again, wounded and treated with contempt.

Merlin has always been more comfortable with and received more love and loyalty from members of the lower classes, the servants. These characters are strong, well-delineated persons. Among them is Moravik, Merlin's nurse from Brittany, long a part of the household and servant to Merlin's mother. Moravik is a warm, motherly, protective woman, yet curious and gossipy; although a Christian, she is superstitious, carrying talismans against the evil eye. She shares Merlin's bedroom when he is a young boy. Since she likes to sit and snooze in the sun, Merlin has opportunities to run off by himself. Then when the other royal children are born, Moravik is needed for the nursery and no longer has charge of Merlin.

The other two servants who are important parts of Merlin's life are Cerdic and Cadal. Cerdic is a Saxon, taken years before in a raid and now one of the grooms, a small man with "bowed legs," "a seamed brown face," and a "thatch of light-coloured hair" (31). He looks after the young boy and dresses his cut cheek with horse liniment when Merlin is struck by his grandfather. It is Cerdic who is killed by Camlach's men when he spills oil that accidentally causes the death of the drunken king.

Later, when Merlin comes to Brittany, Ambrosius assigns Cadal to be his servant and bodyguard. Cadal is a "short stocky man with a square reddish face" and a "black shag of hair" (167). He becomes Merlin's loyal companion through the growing-up years and then stays with him at the Crystal Cave until Uther sends for Merlin. Finally, Cadal, the only friend that Merlin has left, is fatally wounded at Tintagel, a disaster for which Merlin feels responsible. Despite the outcome, Cadal is satisfied with events when Merlin prophesies to him about the coming of Arthur.

Merlin is single-minded once he becomes aware of his powers of sight; he realizes that his visions require particular attention and often action. Galapas tells him: "The gods only go with you, Myrddin Emrys, if you put yourself in their path. And that takes courage" (68). At the moments of their happening, he has "known" of the deaths of first his mother and then Ambrosius. With the visions comes a sense of power and yet humility, as Merlin sees himself as the instrument of the gods, to bring about certain events. He knows, too, that the gods are capricious. They provide the "sight" when it suits them to do so. He cannot command the power or force the visions; they come when they come, and no will of his own can prompt them. Nevertheless, he has the sense of being purposely led in a definite direction.

The youthful Merlin is attracted to a lovely young girl, Keri, and he is almost involved in a relationship but is humiliated out of it. His instincts prevent him from experiencing physical love. Until he is elderly, Merlin has no love relationship. Mary Stewart has suggested that because there is so strong a connection in legend and in history between celibacy or virginity and power, it seemed reasonable to make Merlin celibate.

Mary Stewart gives Merlin's mother the name Niniane, which is the name (with the variations of Vivian and Nimue) that belongs also to the young sorceress who, according to legend, eventually wins Merlin's heart and costs him his powers. Merlin's mother appears only briefly in the story, but one is always aware of her presence in Merlin's thoughts and affections. She loves her son and fears for his safety, first from the anger of her father and then from the ambitions of her brother Camlach. She would like to keep Merlin safe by taking him with her when she goes into the seclusion of St. Peter's, yet even from the beginning she remains withdrawn and leaves Merlin much to himself. When mother and son appear before Vortigern, she is terrified when she realizes his purpose in sending for them, but she maintains composure; she has always displayed the dignity of a princess but has no desire, once her brief love affair is over, to gain a new lover or husband.

Ambrosius is everything that Merlin has wanted in a father. He is a strong character, a born leader, a trained soldier. Once he surmises that Merlin is his son, he treats him like a prince, and it is soon obvious to everyone from the similarity of their features, long before Merlin is aware, that Merlin is Ambrosius's son. Ambrosius sees quickly that Merlin's visions can be useful to him and Uther in their cause, and he would like Merlin to prophesy for him about the immediate future of the campaign against Vortigern. Merlin explains, however, that he cannot prophesy at will. Then without realizing what he has said, Merlin, upon stating that he would have chosen Ambrosius as his father out of everyone he has known, adds, "After all, what boy would not choose the king of all Britain for his father?" (227).

Uther is different from his brother, less sensitive, yet sensual. Women are a necessary part of his life, but until he meets Ygraine he has not become seriously attached. Uther cannot understand Ambrosius's lack of interest in women, and at first he misunderstands his brother's attachment to Merlin, suspecting that Ambrosius may be following the Roman custom of having a young male lover. Although his overwhelming passion for Ygraine eventually causes the death of Gorlois, Uther blames Merlin for what he sees as the needless disaster that follows, and his pride will not allow him to admit his own guilt or accept the idea of a bastard child, a visible symbol of his treachery to Gorlois. By the end of the novel, however, Uther has supposedly achieved everything he wished for.

Ygraine is one of Mary Stewart's strong women, as is Merlin's mother. A beautiful woman coming from a line of kings, she too has dignity and pride; although she silently responds to Uther's passions, she will do nothing to compromise her husband's position. The visit in disguise by Uther and Merlin and two of their men has been arranged but supposedly with no harm involved to Gorlois. In other accounts of this legendary visit, Merlin transforms Uther so that Ygraine believes it is her husband she is receiving. The transformation, in other words, involves magic. In Stewart's version, Merlin is not a magician, although his special gifts allow him to accomplish extraordinary feats. On the visit, the men are hooded and (with the help of hair dye and such, one learns later) have been made to appear like the originals.

Ygraine has said to Merlin as a warning that if he causes bloodshed to come to Cornwall or death to her husband, she will spend the rest of her life praying to any gods there are that he too will die betrayed by a woman. The irony is that in popular legend this is what happens, but in Mary Stewart's version the reality is less dramatic but also more satisfying (see chapter 7).

Merlin's Gods

By the time Merlin is eighteen he has been exposed to several religions. Fifth-century Britain is supposedly predominantly Christian, as is Merlin's grandfather's household, but of the persons close to him, only his mother and Moravik seem to be practicing Christians. In growing up, he has received periodic instruction from the priests. In Wales now, however, where Celtic customs remain the strongest, many Celts still worship their own gods. The Romans earlier were apparently tolerant of these differences, for the Celtic gods shared many characteristics of the Roman gods, and also the Roman presence was less dominant in Wales. Despite the increasing power of Christianity, Merlin is attuned most of all to the Celtic gods, the gods of the hills, the caves, of nature. About the countryside there are carved wooden figures of these deities.

Merlin finds one by the Crystal Cave, the area that becomes home. Galapas, living in the cave, has the greatest influence on Merlin, becoming teacher, friend, and father figure. Because they share the gift of vision, Merlin communicates with Galapas on a more meaningful plane than he has ever been able to do with anyone else. To Merlin, the whole fabric of his existence is interwoven with the gods or god; he is never sure whether there are many gods or various aspects of one major god, but he wants to investigate, to learn. At one point, Merlin tells Cadal that there is nothing in the world that he is not ready to see and learn and no god that he is "not ready to approach in his own fashion." He says also that truth is "the shadow of God" and that if he is to use truth, he must know who God is. When Cadal asks which god he is talking about, Merlin answers, "I think there is only one. Oh, there are gods everywhere, in the hollow hills, in the wind and the sea, in the very grass we walk on and the air we breathe, and in the bloodstained shadows where men like Belasius wait for them. But I believe there must be one who is God himself, like the great sea, and all the rest of us, small gods and men and all, like rivers, we all come to Him in the end" (216–17). But Merlin never seriously questions the nature of the deity; he is content (as far as the reader knows) to receive him or them and be the instrument for the shaping of important events. The gods in their own way have carried him to Brittany to his father and have helped him assist Ambrosius in the taking of Britain and then the real task of arranging events for the coming of Arthur.

The experience with the Druids, however, is alien to Merlin and his psyche. Merlin knows that this priestly caste of the Celts has been outlawed but continues to practice secretly in isolated areas. Not long after he comes to Brittany, when he is riding in the forest with Cadal, he hears a scream and goes off by himself to investigate the source; he comes upon the Druid ritual of human sacrifice, a part of which he witnesses at a distance. Shortly thereafter he encounters his tutor Belasius, the Druid archpriest who tries to frighten Merlin with a curse if he tells. About what he has seen, Merlin is repulsed, yet intensely curious. He admits to Ambrosius that he has seen the Druids and discovers that Ambrosius knows Belasius's secret but has retained him as tutor because of his mathematical and astronomical talents. Part of Merlin's lack of fear in certain situations comes from his prophetic confidence in what he instinctively knows will come about, but his "knowing" is limited.

Another incidence of Merlin's ability to experience the gods comes with his exposure to the third religion in the area. Merlin at age twelve has just escaped from the ship bringing him to Brittany and has been hiding in the stable, cold and hungry. Then he has a vision in which he sees a man in strange dress in a field, approaching a white bull. After the bull charges, the man ropes the animal and overpowers it, skillfully slitting its throat. Merlin finds himself running into the field to help the man but suddenly awakens and discovers that he is surrounded by strange men. This is his first encounter with Ambrosius. The men are flabbergasted when he describes what he saw, which appears to have been a vision of Mithras himself. Ambrosius, Uther, and their men, including most of the soldiers, are followers of the god Mithras. According to Persian legend, Mithras releases the forces of life by slaying a huge bull, and the god is representative of both light and life. Mithraism was a religion held by many Romans but open only to men. Christians deplored the beliefs of this group because they followed closely the customs of Christianity. Mithras, it was said, was born on Christmas Day, December twenty-fifth, and the central ritual of his worship was a shared meal; standards of conduct also resembled those of the Christians.

Merlin also becomes familiar with some of the secret rites of this masked group when, years later, he is invited to attend and take part in ceremonies with his father and Uther. Ambrosius tells Merlin: "As you will find, all gods who are born of the light are brothers, and in this land, if Mithras who gives us victory is to bear the face of Christ, why, then, we worship Christ" (390). Merlin has not broken the vow of secrecy regarding the rites. He says of himself that he has never escaped the spell of the secret god who led him to Brittany and to his father. But he does not know which god this is, nor is it allowable to question his identity.

Additional Notes

Although as Mary Stewart says, she received her story line from Geoffrey of Monmouth's *The History of the Kings of Britain,* her imagination took creative leaps. The places she talks about are authentic, but she invented the cave of Galapas (the Crystal Cave), although one would find in Wales in the area on that particular hill, Bryn Myrddin, a well and a burial mound at the top of the hill. Geoffrey mentions the Galabes springs where Merlin was often seen.

Another important connection that Stewart chose to expand was the relationship between Merlin and Ambrosius, which seems to have had no basis in legend, although Nennius, a ninth-century historian who influenced Geoffrey's material, called the prophet "Ambrosius" and provided the story of the dragons in the pool. Geoffrey's account assumes that Merlin is also called Ambrosius; as Stewart says, this information gave her "the idea of identifying the 'prince of darkness' who fathered Merlin" and suggested the main plot of *The Crystal Cave.*[5]

There are many ways in which Geoffrey's *History* is different from Stewart's novel. In his version are several pages of unrelated prophecies given by Merlin at the time of the dragons-in-the-pool incident. Further, his white dragon symbolizes the Saxons and the red, the people of Britain, and the Saxons are responsible for the deaths of both Ambrosius and Uther by poisoning. In Geoffrey's version Merlin is not Ambrosius's son. In the incident with Ygraine, she is deceived into thinking that the "transformed" Uther is her husband, and the child born (Arthur) is not spirited away but accepted by Uther. In addition, in Geoffrey's account both Merlin and Ambrosius are Christians.

The Symbol of the Cave

The symbol of the cave has been prominent in the myths of the gods through the ages. Zeus, Dionysius, Hermes, Apollo, and Mithras were either born in or closely connected with a cave. The cave has been the symbol of the womb of Mother Earth and was important also in the Celtic worship, the hollow hills being the link to the otherworld. In Stewart's story Merlin, too, is conceived in a cave.

Plato's cave was the symbol of darkness and ignorance from which man emerged into the light of truth and knowledge, and therefore the cave was to be transcended. This is not what happens with Merlin or for those who see the cave as a sacred dwelling, for Merlin retreats into the cave when his work is done, going back to Mother Earth. The three books of Merlin, *The Crystal Cave*, *The Hollow Hills*, and *The Last Enchantment* are (as their titles indicate) closely connected with the influence of the particular cave with which Merlin identifies. His powers are, he believes, closely allied to the god (or gods) who are identified with the sacred cave, and from this affiliation he gains strength.

In legend, the sacred cave of Merlin is seen as a place where a demonic spirit born of a woman and a devil prophesies about the future. The view of Merlin as the son of Satan persisted. In most instances, however, he is not seen as an evil force, and his influence on those around him is for the good of Arthur and of Britain.

Chapter Six

The Arthurian Novels:
Merlin and the Young Arthur

The Hollow Hills

The Hollow Hills (1973) covers the early years of Arthur's life, from his conception and supposed date of birth (about 470) to the beginning of his kingship, shortly before his fourteenth birthday (about 484). As Mary Stewart says, "This story is of a period of Arthur's life which tradition barely touches, and history not at all."[1]

It continues the events of *The Crystal Cave* and opens the day after the fateful visit to Tintagel by King Uther and Merlin and their men. Despite the chronological connection, Mary Stewart wanted *The Hollow Hills* to be independent of *The Crystal Cave,* maintaining that it should stand on its own. The first few chapters, therefore, include skillfully integrated background information to bring the reader up to date.

Merlin continues as the narrator, and his humanness is immediately emphasized because he has been severely wounded in the previous evening's bitter fight to the death. As he awakens, lying on the ground among the bushes, the first person he encounters is a young boy, a goatherd, who views him with a heavy stick in his hand. Is Merlin to be robbed and beaten? He is helpless and knows he could not fend off an attack, but luckily the boy, who first thought him dead, only hopes for a reward for catching Merlin's horse. He tells the boy about what happened the previous night and, purposely, one discovers, pretends that the king and his companions had been magically changed to look like Duke Gorlois and his men so that the people allowing entry to the castle and especially Ygraine would remain blameless.

Merlin knows how the tales of his wizardry grow and become exaggerated by the common people. He introduces himself now as the king's nephew, "Merlin the Enchanter." The frightened boy runs off as quickly as he can, taking time only to pick up the gold coin Merlin throws to him.

Merlin's vulnerability is also seen almost immediately after this incident, as he leans painfully against his horse. The king comes riding back to Tintagel with his men, and although they pass by Merlin, the king does not acknowledge him. Today the king looks like himself again, the gray dye washed from his hair and beard. Merlin realizes that he is to be the public sacrifice for the remorse and guilt Uther feels for the death of Duke Gorlois and the needless haste to possess the duke's wife. As narrator, Merlin is thoroughly sympathetic. His fears and concerns are mainly for others, since his mission is to secure the infant Arthur from harm and then protect him over the years from the enemies anxious to destroy him. In one sense, this novel is a gigantic version of the suspense-story chase, except that here the pursuit goes on less conspicuously for the duration of most of the novel. In *The Hollow Hills,* many unknown but possible pursuers provide the resulting tension and suspense.

The Plot

After the wounded Merlin is cared for and healed by the king's physician, Gandar, whom he has known since boyhood, Merlin goes back to the Crystal Cave. He feels his god has deserted him. Not long after, he rescues Ralf, grandson of Marcia, the queen's trusted servant and confidante. Marcia has sent the boy to be with Merlin, for Ralf, too, is in disgrace with the king for aiding the visitors that night at Tintagel. It becomes obvious that Merlin is being watched, but he doesn't know by whom. Is it Cador, son of the Duke of Gorlois, hoping for revenge?

Word comes that the queen, now expecting a child, wishes to see Merlin secretly; thus, disguised as an eye doctor, Merlin, with Ralf as his assistant, makes the journey back to Tintagel. Ygraine asks Merlin to take the baby when he is born and hide him. On the way back, Merlin and Ralf take pains to avoid the king's troops, but as they accidentally meet the king's men, Merlin learns that the king has just sent for him. Uther makes the same request as Ygraine. He had planned to send the baby to King Budec in Brittany for protection, but Budec has just died; therefore he asks Merlin to provide a solution. Merlin wants to take the baby to his own former nurse, Moravik, now living in Brittany, and when the infant is four years old, he will bring him back to Britain for secret care. Uther is relieved, for he wants the child out of the way, believing that he will have additional sons, one of whom will become king.

Merlin is present at the Christmas birth. Ygraine has named the baby Arthur and requests that he be baptized as a Christian. Disguised as a musician, Merlin, together with Ralf, the baby, and a young court servant, Branwen, as wet nurse, sails for Brittany and the court of King Hoel, Budec's son. In the northern part of Hoel's lands is the village of Coll, where Moravik and her husband have a tavern. As Merlin and his party travel through the Perilous Forest, unescorted to keep from being noticed, they are almost beset by robbers but are saved by a white deer that suddenly appears and draws the men's attention. Merlin brings the baby safely to the waiting Moravik; Branwen and Ralf are to remain with the infant.

Now Merlin is free to go where he pleases but not back to Britain or near Arthur. He knows that enemies will try to find the baby by locating him. Merlin therefore travels to Italy and the Near East for the next four years, working also for a time in a hospital in Italy. He keeps in touch with King Hoel and in the firelight has limited visions of Ralf and the group at Coll. He has arranged for the group to leave Brittany when Arthur is four, and the party is met by Count Ector in northern Britain, where Arthur is to remain for the next ten years. Although rumors abound, no one else knows where the young Arthur is or if he is still living.

Two more years pass, and then Merlin realizes from a dream/vision that it is time to go home. In Constantinople he sees a mosaic of the sword of Maximus, a vision that has appeared to him several times. Word from Count Ector is that the military situation is serious. The Saxons are planning another big invasion, and the Angles have been conspiring to use the harbors of the Picts to the north for an invasion there. Uther has been unwell for some time and wants Merlin's assistance, especially as the question of succession has become of utmost importance.

When Merlin arrives in Britain, he reassures Uther that he is not dying. Uther, who has become temporarily impotent from a wound that would not heal, is suffering a depression caused partly by the stillborn birth of a son. Earlier a daughter had been born to Uther and Ygraine. The one living son has now become crucial, and Merlin discloses to Uther where Arthur is living. The king had not inquired before.

Uther recovers, and Merlin goes back to the Crystal Cave with his servant Stilicho, whom he has brought from Italy. With evidence that he is being watched and is in danger, Merlin leaves on a northern route by off-the-road trails through the forests. At one point he is captured by the forest people, who have been told to look for him; Merlin speaks their language and quickly makes them his allies. In a nearby village close to Ector's lands, he visits a smithy who gives him information about the sword of the great Maximus, which had been brought back from Rome a hundred years before. Following mystical clues, Merlin travels to Segontium, one of the former homes of Maximus.

In the ruins of a tower in a shrine, under an altar dedicated to Mithras, Merlin finds the great sword. Traveling again to Ector's land, he comes upon a chapel at the edge of a forest. The hermit priest, suffering from a stroke, dies, and Merlin then realizes that this is the ideal hiding place. He will become the keeper of the chapel. The people in the village will not be curious but will accept him as a holy man, and he can contact Count Ector nearby. Merlin hides the sword in a cave on a small, supposedly enchanted island, Caer Bannog, in a lake he has ridden by many times.

The first appearance of the nine-year-old Arthur comes as he is riding furiously through the woods, trying to outrun Ralf. He has visited the chapel before, when Prosper, the former holy man, lived here. Now as they meet, Arthur does not know Merlin, nor has he known his own identity; Ralf, on the other hand, is delighted to see Merlin but he must hide his enthusiasm, and they converse secretly. Later, when Merlin visits Ector's castle, Ector brings him up to date on Arthur's past five years. Bedwyr, who is the son of King Bannock and is Arthur's age, is living temporarily in Ector's household, and the boys become great friends. Ector's own son Cei also comes with the boys at first, as they visit the hermit of the Green Chapel. When Bedwyr has gone home again, Arthur spends many hours with Merlin. He has heard stories of the hidden prince and of the magician Merlin.

The year after Arthur's thirteenth birthday is known as the Black Year. Saxon invasions are imminent and cold weather cripples crops, leading to sickness and starvation. Another threat is that King Lot in the North wants to become High King and has contracted several years before to marry twelve-year-old Morgian, Uther's daughter, at the coming Christmas. Because Uther's health is poor, he is urged to name an heir.

One day as Merlin is fishing in the lake opposite the island of Caer Bannog, Arthur on his new white horse comes racing by, his white hound (Cabal) chasing a white stag that jumps into the water and crosses to the island. The hound follows, and though Arthur is hesitant to approach the forbidden island, he wants to retrieve his dog. At Merlin's suggestion, Arthur leaves his horse and takes the small boat tied nearby to bring him back. Merlin's "vision" allows him to see Arthur as he enters the cave and discovers the sword. Excitedly, Arthur brings it back with the dog. At this moment Cador, son of Gorlois and now Duke of Cornwall, appears with his troops. He has been searching for Merlin. Tension mounts as Merlin tries to protect Arthur's identity, and Arthur, assuming harm to Merlin, springs to his aid.

When Merlin sends Arthur and the captured Ralf to the chapel to wait for him, one finds that Cador has come as a friend, urging that Merlin send Arthur to the king as the one strong claim that can bind the kingdom together; otherwise, Lot's followers will force the other nobles to name Lot as heir. It has been rumored that Lot, King of Lothian and Orkney, has made overtures to the Saxons. The expected Saxon attacks will come from the north and east; the king's troops have already ridden north to Luguvallium, where the battle is expected. Merlin quickly agrees to join Cador with Arthur that evening at Ector's castle, and then they will meet the king. When Merlin and Arthur are alone, Merlin answers Arthur's questions about the identity of the sword, adding that it must wait here to be claimed by the legitimate heir to the kingdom. Then he identifies himself as Merlin the Enchanter. Arthur is astounded but does not yet guess that he himself is the hidden prince. Uther had requested earlier that he be the one to tell him.

Next, a troop of the king's men appears with Uther's summons that Merlin come as he used to for his father Ambrosius, to provide strength and help to Uther's army. When the men have gone, Merlin surprises Arthur by producing a magical fire and places the sword into the altar, which before has held only the stony likeness of the sword. Arthur is then elated to learn that he will join the troops and fight with the king.

By the time Merlin and Arthur, with escort, reach Luguvallium, the king's forces are already drawing up battle stations. When the men see Merlin, they shout his name and he in turn indicates they will be victorious. King Uther is carried into battle in a chair/litter, calling for Arthur to be by his side. Arthur, in white, is immediately conspicuous. The battle is won, but at one point Arthur, fighting hard, loses his sword and the king throws him his. Arthur charges forward fearlessly, inspiring the others. Lot, waiting on the side to see whom the battle would favor, sends his troops in when the battle is already won.

Later Merlin aids with the medical units, and Morgause, the king's twenty-one-year-old bastard daughter, helps with the wounded. Arthur visits them there, elated over the day's events.

When Merlin meets with the king, he can see that Uther's death is near, and the king asks Merlin to stay by Arthur, to guide and guard him. When Merlin returns, he finds Arthur missing. His forebodings are justified when he discovers that Arthur has been lured into Morgause's room and into lovemaking. She knows that Arthur is her half-brother and that she will gain power by influencing him and, as Merlin can foresee, by carrying his child, the child who will one day cause Arthur's death.

Merlin is forced to tell Arthur now that the king is his father and Morgause his half-sister; later when Arthur meets with the king, Merlin orders Morgause to leave the court forever. At the victory feast, Uther proclaims Arthur his heir but is challenged by Lot and his followers; moreover, the king's sword is mysteriously broken when it is to be presented to Arthur. In the anger and confusion that follow, the king dies, but Ector and others speak up for Arthur, and Merlin promises that the next morning at the chapel Arthur will receive his real sword.

To avoid foul play, Merlin leaves by himself as quickly as possible for the chapel. But two of Lot's men have gone ahead, laying a trap for Merlin, and Merlin must fight for his life. He is wounded but found unconscious and saved by the forest people. In the morning the crowd gathers at the chapel as Merlin again produces the mysterious fire and Arthur draws forth the great sword from the altar of stone. At this sign, all kneel and are ready to swear allegiance. Arthur's speech to the people gives them additional assurance that he is their proper leader.

Structure

Throughout the novel there is uneven pacing, but much of that is dictated by the nature of the plot. *The Hollow Hills* is divided into four sections. Book I, called "The Waiting," is the largest section, covering one-third of the story; it could have been a complete novel in itself. "The Waiting," of course refers to the period leading up to the birth of the baby and the infant's being hidden safely in his first permanent home with Moravik in Brittany.

This has been a difficult time for Merlin. He is alone, in disfavor with the king, and depressed because the gods seem to have deserted him, and he fears that everything he has done may be the result of a dream or possibly a mockery. By the time both Ygraine and Uther have each asked him to take the baby, he is reassured that events are working out as he had foreseen in his vision.

He finds the same great star in the sky on the night of the birth of the Christmas baby as on the death previously of his father Ambrosius. By establishing the baby Arthur with the same signs as those of the Christ child, Stewart gives the infant a supernatural aura, but the parallel is not objectionable. In the Perilous Forest, Branwen, calmly riding on the mule, carrying the baby, reminds one also of Mary carrying the Christ child. As they are about to be discovered by the two outlaws, the white hind appears, seemingly from nowhere, distracting the men and leading them in the opposite direction. By the end of Book I, Merlin, in a dream, sees in the sky the jewel-like sword that moves downward toward a giant standing stone, eventually sliding into the stone. Merlin takes this as a sign that his god is with him again. Despite the supernatural touches, the elements of fantasy are not emphasized.

Book II of *The Hollow Hills,* entitled "The Search," is the most slow-moving section. It covers six years, whereas Book I covers only ten months. Here, there is little action and little suspense. Merlin is again waiting out the time until it is safe to return to Britain. In one sense it is a happy time, for he is free of obligations and free to travel to the lands he has always heard about. For the reader, this section may represent a slump. Not until Merlin gets back to the Crystal Cave and then heads north toward Ector's lands does he receive the signs that begin the actual search for the Sword of Maximus. During all this time in Britain, however, Merlin himself is the object of a search and must actively stay hidden. This section ends as Merlin brings back the sword and finds the chapel with the dying hermit.

Book III, entitled "The Sword," is the shortest section, but it covers approximately five years. The pace of the novel accelerates here again. The section begins with Merlin's burying the holy man at the Green Chapel and his decision to remain as keeper; it includes Arthur's appearance, his visits with Bedwyr, and his finding the sword on the isle of Caer Bannog; and it concludes with the appearance of Cador's and the king's troops summoning them and with Merlin's disguising the real sword on the stone altar.

Book IV, entitled, "The King," is also a short section, filled with action, suspense, and rapid pacing and covering three days. It begins with the assembling of the troops ready to do battle and ends with the acceptance of Arthur as king. It also includes, however, Merlin's battle with the two men, followers of Lot, intent on murdering him. This is another instance of Merlin's vulnerability but also of his courage, intelligence, and ability to cope with ugly, physical situations. The fight scene here parallels Merlin's battle with Brithnael at the end of *The Crystal Cave*.

Shades of the Grail Legend

Although much that Mary Stewart creates in *The Hollow Hills* is fantasy, the references to the life of Magnus Maximus are fact. Of Spanish origin, Maximus was a Roman emperor who married a British princess and came to live in Britain. He was proclaimed emperor of Britain in 383 by his soldiers and held much of Western Europe for some years with mainly British troops. He led his forces against Rome and held it for a time but was defeated and killed in 388 by the Emperor of the East, Theodosius. Many of the Britons who served with him later settled in Gaul or Brittany. Others came back to Britain.

As Geoffrey Ashe says of Maximus, "He lives on in the traditions of later ages as Prince Macsen, a hero of Welsh and Cornish folklore. Because of his adventure, the British sense of identity grew stronger."[2] It is the sword of Maximus that Mary Stewart has created, a sword that in this story was brought back to Britain by the followers of Maximus a hundred years before Arthur's time and then supposedly lost. It is this sword that Merlin sees images of and feels compelled to find for the glory of the coming king. At Segontium in the ruins of Macsen's Tower, Merlin locates the sword. He has received signs aiding him in his search, one of which comes from the dying hermit of the Green Chapel as he relates what is said about the stone altar and the sword. Although some of Maximus's men were followers of Mithras, most were Christians, and in their makeshift devotion in the small chapel, they stood the sword against the bare altar to form a cross and from their treasures took a Greek-style grail, large and deep, from which they drank. One of the men fashioned, with hammer and chisel, a stone sword into the altar. The men then left, taking with them the real sword and the grail. One day, it was said, the original sword would come back to the shrine and stand there for a cross.

When Merlin brings back the sword, however, he hides it on the mysterious isle of Caer Bannog until it is time for Arthur to find it. "Search" and "grail" legends stem from ancient folklore. The most familiar of these, that of the Holy Grail identified with the Last Supper, originated largely in twelfth-century versions of the earlier Celtic quest stories. The Holy Grail romances developed as a part of the Arthurian legend in France, and among the Grail seekers were Percival, Gawain, Lancelot, and Galahad, all Arthurian knights. Here, however, it is not the grail but the sword that is the object of the quest.

Mary Stewart gives Arthur characteristics typical of the searcher. Usually the searcher, like Arthur, is an unknown youth, brought up in seclusion, ignorant of his name or parentage. Traditionally he comes across a wasteland ruled by a maimed, impotent king. In this case the maimed king might be Uther and the devastated land is Britain. Usually there is a castle on a small island; in Stewart's novel there is a rock formation that in certain lights looks like a castle, and *Caer Bannog* means "The Castle in the Mountains." The searcher reaches the island by boat, as does Arthur. The island in legend is said to be owned by the King of the Underworld; Here, the people believe it is haunted by Bilis, the dwarf king of the otherworld. In some versions a white stag leads the searcher to the goal, as happens here with Arthur, when his dog Cabal chases the white stag. On the return of the searcher, "fertility and peace are restored to the wasteland";[3] here, the result of Arthur's kingship is to be eventually a time of comparative peace and harmony.

Characterization

Mary Stewart sees Merlin "as the link between the worlds; the instrument by which, as he says, 'all the kings become one king and all the gods one God.' For this he abnegates his own will and his desire for normal manhood. The hollow hills are the physical point of entry between this world and the Otherworld, and Merlin is their human counterpart, the meeting point for the interlocking worlds of men, gods, beasts and twilight spirits" (399).

Once Merlin has seen that he is not deserted by his god, he does not offer to blaspheme him by further questioning. In fact, he has a liberal approach. When he arrives at the Green Chapel, the dying holy man asks Merlin if he also is a Christian. Merlin answers indirectly, "I serve God," he says (235). The holy man has been aware of the other spirits and wonders if he did wrong in shutting them out. As he wants to view the altar again, Merlin reconstructs the vision by concentrating on the fire, but the original name of Mithras does not appear with the rest of the altar inscription. This is the first indication that the Christian God may be dominant. Yet when Merlin has become the keeper of the shrine, he decides to open it to any god that would care to use it. He thus uncovers the cloth from Mithras's altar and lights the nine bronze lamps for the Celtic gods, declaring an open house to all.

At the end of the novel, however, after the nobles have accepted Arthur and all has been done, Merlin carries the nine lamps out of the chapel and will take them where he says they now belong, "up to the caves of the hollow hills where their gods had gone" (392). During the fiery transformation of the sword, the lamps have been overturned, the oil spilled, and the stone bowl shattered; all that has been left is the wording on the hilt of the sword, To Him Unconquered. One assumes, then, that the time has come and the Christian God has at last made himself visible.

In this novel the facet of Merlin that one hasn't seen before is Merlin the singer. He becomes that briefly as a disguise on the trip to Brittany, but he is apparently a talented bard; he had first been taught to play the harp and to sing by his grandfather's young (third) wife (in *The Crystal Cave*). Later in Brittany, as he was growing up, he practiced, we are told, in the evenings so that now he is able to entertain creditably King Hoel's nobles and also the cruder audience at the tavern in Coll where he arrives with Ralf, Branwen, and the baby.

Ralf has turned from a sullen boy, when he is first sent by his grandmother to Merlin's care, into a responsible, loyal, and courageous young man. He becomes devoted to Merlin and then to Arthur, seeming to thrive on the dangers encountered in his travels with Merlin. He has come to admire Merlin's apparent fearlessness and adaptability. Merlin's first visit from Ralf reminds one of Robinson Crusoe's first view of his man Friday. From his lonely hillside, Merlin can see in the distance a man being attacked by others. The victim seems to be getting away, but before the men can further pursue him they are diverted and ride away. Merlin quickly goes to the rescue of the wounded Ralf; thereafter Ralf becomes his servant and companion until it is time to guard the infant Arthur in Brittany and then remove with him to Count Ector's castle in northern Britain. Ralf's responsibility lasts through the years and even into Arthur's first battle. Ralf remains near, ready to defend him.

When Cador, Duke of Cornwall, first sees Arthur, he is impressed with Arthur's readiness to attack to defend Merlin until it is evident that Cador is not an enemy. Cador says to Merlin, "Did you know he was more like you than ever like the king?" (302). In fact, one discovers later that Arthur suspects that Merlin may be his father. He does not find out the truth until after the unfortunate affair with Morgause, when Merlin says of himself that he has been celibate all his life. Merlin, even on his first meeting with Arthur, recognizes an important difference between himself and the boy. He, at Arthur's age, "had been content with very little," not guessing his power. Arthur, Merlin sees, "would never be content with less than all." Arthur is tall, "sturdily built," giving the "impression of a blazing controlled vitality" (257).

Arthur is eager to join the troops in battle and has been frustrated that Ector has not taken him along on previous campaigns. He is confident and, in his white trappings, as they assemble for battle, has all eyes upon him. Some of the troops may guess that he is the long-absent prince, Uther's heir, but most do not yet know his identity. Mary Stewart's Arthur is a human, likeable young man. He has a strong friendship with Bedwyr, who idolizes Arthur and follows his lead. In later legends Bedwyr's name is changed to Bedivere; as Stewart points out, he seems to be the original of Lancelot, and one finds this likeness in her version of the role in the next novel, *The Last Enchantment*.

The characters in this novel tend to fall into two groups: the friends and the enemies, or the good versus the evil. Uther for some time is a shadowy figure. Merlin is not sure of the extent of Uther's anger and guilt, but with failing health and no more sons, Uther becomes increasingly dependent on Merlin's cooperation and the necessity to produce Arthur as his heir; still, Merlin is painfully aware that Uther does not "like" him.

Among the "good" characters is Ygraine, mother of Arthur. One sees her fleetingly in this novel, only when she summons Merlin to ask him to take the baby. Ector and Drusilla are the thoroughly reliable, steadfast, loyal couple, Christians, delighted to have Arthur live with them and become a second son. Ector takes seriously his commitment to guide, teach, protect, and love this boy, whose enemies would kill him if they could find him. Bedwyr, along with his father, King of Benoic, is also among the good people. It is Bedwyr who gives the white hound Cabal to Arthur as a present and a major reason that Arthur is determined not to lose the dog as it chases the white stag.

The evil characters, the enemies of Arthur and Merlin, include Lot, who is suspected of making deals with the Saxons. His ambitions to be High King have already caused him to make the marriage contract to wed Princess Morgian. He risks losing Uther's favor by waiting to see how the fighting will go before entering the crucial battle. He is the most outspoken challenger to Arthur's kingship and is also responsible, it appears, for the king's broken sword and for ordering his men to waylay Merlin before the ceremony of the sword.

Cador has seemed an enemy from the beginning of this novel and was so at first. As the son of Gorlois, he has reason to hate both Uther and Merlin. At several points in the novel, it is Cador's men, as Merlin suspects, that are trying to find and harm Merlin for revenge. Later, however, Cador becomes an associate of Uther, loyal to him, and as the Duke of Cornwall and a practical man, anxious that the kingdom remain undivided and free of Saxons. Until almost the end, however, Merlin sees Cador as a threat to both himself and Arthur.

Distinctive Prose

As in the other novels, Mary Stewart's descriptions are striking. Her scenes appeal to the senses, and among the favorite poetic techniques is alliteration. In the following scene Merlin is standing in deep sorrow at the foot of the bier of Duke Gorlois. Gorlois was a friend of his father's, a loyal man, trusting Merlin.

Slowly, all through the fortress, I could hear the sounds dwindling and sinking to silence as men finally went to rest. The sea soughed and beat below the window. The wind plucked at the wall, and ferns growing there in the crevices rustled and tapped. A rat scuttled and squeaked somewhere. The resin bubbled in the torches. Sweet and foul, through the sharp smoke, I smelled the smell of death. The torchlight winked blank and flat from the coins on the dead eyes. (18)

He sees someone then, a guard he believes, moving restlessly, scraping his spear on the stone floor. Then he sees the eyes and recognizes the fierce-looking young warrior: "With a shock that went through me like the spear striking I recognized them. Gorlois' eyes. It was Gorlois' son Cador of Cornwall, who stood between me and the dead, watching me steadily, with hatred" (19).

In almost all descriptive passages Stewart includes sounds and smells as well as visual stimuli. She chooses vibrant verbs and earthy images. The quoted lines show her fondness for alliteration—here, noticeably, with the *s* sounds. The poetic techniques, however, are never intrusive. Her poet's ear is reliable.

In *The Hollow Hills* as in the suspense novels, the fight scenes are remarkably realistic, not sparing of the grim details, but there are, too, spots of humor throughout the story. These occur mainly in dialogue, Merlin's comments to others that show a willingness to laugh at himself. The humor comes as comic relief, usually after a particularly trying experience.

For example, after the unplanned meeting with the king, Merlin and Ralf, previously in disguise, are relieved when the king seeks Merlin's assistance with the coming baby. The tensions have been strong and their travels harrowing. Merlin says (now that the danger has passed), "By all the living gods, I'm glad that things are moving now. And gladder for the moment of one thing more than any other." Ralf asks, "That you're to get the child so easily?" Merlin answers, "Oh, that, of course. No, I really meant that now at last I can shave off this damnable beard" (88–89).

Another touch of humor follows the disguised Merlin's evening of entertaining for tone-deaf King Hoel's nobles. As he shows Ralf the silver and gold pieces and the jewel given him, Merlin assures Ralf that he did indeed sing to them. He says, "It's nice to think, isn't it, that one can earn one's keep so handsomely?" He adds, "The jewel was from the King, a bribe to stop me singing, otherwise they'd have had me there yet" (117).

Yet another notable moment of humor occurs at the end of Cador's suspenseful visit, just after Arthur has appeared with the newfound sword. Arthur will remain with Merlin that evening before they go off to join the king's forces. Cador offers Merlin a horse to go back to the chapel, but Merlin, who has been fishing, says that he will walk back when he is ready, for there is something he has to do first. When Cador asks what it is, Merlin replies, "I still have to catch my dinner, and for two now, instead of one. . . . If Arthur can lift the sword of Maximus from the lake, surely I shall be granted at least two decent fish?" (304).

Chapter Seven

The Arthurian Novels: Merlin and Arthur the King

The Last Enchantment

The Last Enchantment (1979) begins a few hours after the ending of *The Hollow Hills*, later in that same day when Arthur has taken the miraculous sword from the white, heatless fire on the stone altar and been proclaimed king. Merlin, the teller of the story, carries on the narration, reviewing past events; his opening statement, however, is guaranteed to shock the reader into attention. Merlin says: "Not every king would care to start his reign with the wholesale massacre of children. This is what they whisper of Arthur, even though in other ways he is held up as the type itself of the noble ruler, the protector alike of high and lowly."[1]

This Herod-like action is left unresolved until the later sections of Book I, although Merlin defends Arthur and indicates that the blame falls on King Lot and Morgause, Arthur's half-sister. As in the other works, Mary Stewart is expert at building suspense and keeping the reader involved. This novel is episodic, however, rather than building to a central climax as in *The Hollow Hills*, where all action leads to the crowning of the young Arthur. Here the major events are chronological but separate and independent of one another, although the story continues to be that of Merlin and Arthur but Merlin in particular.

The Plot

At King Uther's funeral, the young Arthur meets his mother, Ygraine, for the first time. Later, on his way to Caerleon, Merlin sees in a vision that Morgause and King Lot have been lovers, and she now takes her sister Morgan's place as Lot's bride (in the previous novel Stewart calls Morgan "Morgian").

After Arthur is crowned king at Caerleon, he sends Merlin to Dunpeldyr, King Lot's city, for information about his child. Merlin, traveling in disguise again as an eye doctor with Ulfin, Arthur's servant, meets on the way Beltane, a traveling jeweler, with his assistant, Ninian. Ninian's subsequent death by drowning affects Merlin deeply, for he had hoped to teach the boy many of his own skills.

In Dunpeldyr, Morgause has given birth to a boy. Lot has been absent for several months and now comes home in a fury, having been told that Morgause's child is not his but Arthur's; purposely taunted by Morgause, Lot kills the child but, finding that Morgause has "switched" babies, orders that all newborn infants in the city be put to death. Morgause pretends that this order came from Arthur, since she wants to harm him. Merlin cannot stop the massacre (actually, setting the children adrift in a boat at sea), but he remains in Dunpeldyr for a time, feeling sure now that Morgause has earlier sent the child away to safety. But he learns nothing.

Merlin then plies his talents as engineer to supervise the building and fortifying of the hilltop village of Caer Camel, and Arthur, in constant skirmishes with the Saxon enemy, establishes a finely trained cavalry with imported horses from Spain and with his most trusted men, among them Bedwyr and Cei. Arthur then marries the fifteen-year-old Guenever, one of Ygraine's attendants.

Merlin is asked to escort Arthur's sister Morgan north to wed King Urbgen of Rheged, whom she has come to admire and who is a loyal ally to Arthur. Morgause comes to her sister's wedding and at the feast drugs Merlin's drink and then poisons the wine he takes with him on the way home. The two military escorts do their best to help Merlin and do save him from dying, but deranged, he eludes them and for the next seven months wanders in a wooded wilderness, often aided and cared for by the Old Ones of the forest, the older Celts that have survived in the forests since the days of the Romans. Finally Arthur finds Merlin and brings him to Count Ector's castle to recover. Arthur has changed much in the meantime. In addition to worrying over Merlin, he has had the heartbreak of having Guenever, his young wife, die in a miscarriage; his mother, who had been seriously ill for some time, has also died.

In a recent battle, one finds, Lot has been killed, and Arthur must make arrangements for a successor. He hopes now to make friends of some of the disloyal kings that had been Lot's allies in the North.

Still feeling the effects of his illness, Merlin, back in Caer Camel (called Camelot), builds a house nearby. He knows that Arthur relies on him less now, yet he can be at hand when he is needed. Four more years have elapsed, years of battles with the Saxons, Eosa and Cerdic. It is seven years altogether, with twelve major battles, before the country is at peace.

Four years after the death of Guenever, Arthur's advisers and knights urge him to remarry, and one of his men speaks eloquently of the Princess Guinevere of Northgalis. Arrangements are made with Bedwyr, Melwas, a neighboring king, and others to escort the bride-to-be to Caerleon. Arthur has never met her before, but his reaction is apparently similar to that of Merlin, who is impressed by her beauty and winsome personality. Arthur is obviously devoted to his Guinevere, but in the next few years he is also much occupied with the problems of making the kingdom secure, building fortifications at strategic points and engaging in skirmishes with the Saxons. Threats of large-scale invasions from the Continent continue but with decreasing frequency.

One morning while Arthur is away, Queen Guinevere and two of her ladies ride in the forest as they often do; then suddenly Guinevere is gone. Rescue efforts fail to find her. Hours later Cei, Ector's son, who is in charge of the household while Arthur is gone, comes to Merlin for help. In a vision Merlin sees that Guinevere is held in King Melwas's hunting lodge, but it appears to be a rendezvous, for both are laughing and playing chess and signs indicate they may be lovers. Merlin, anxious to keep the incident quiet, goes with Bedwyr to retrieve Guinevere. Melwas hurries back to his stronghold island as Arthur's ship is sighted in the harbor. Melwas now pretends he rescued Guinevere when she was thrown from her horse in the dangerous, ditch-covered area. Guinevere, however, tells Arthur that Melwas ambushed her and carried her off, and Arthur is convinced she is telling the truth; Merlin finds then that he was wrong in doubting her. It is imperative that Melwas remain an ally, but not long after, Arthur finds an occasion to fight with Melwas in single combat. Arthur wins, and the wounded Melwas again becomes a loyal follower.

Merlin has now acquired a young helper whom he calls Ninian, in memory of the boy who had drowned years before, and to Ninian he passes on many of his skills. This young person also has the power of "sight" and is able to tell Arthur of a vision of piracy in the North that Arthur investigates and finds true. Merlin then discovers, because Arthur tells him, that his young assistant is a girl. Her name is Nimue, she tells Merlin, and she has pretended to be a boy because she knows Merlin would not have let her work with him had he known otherwise.

Both Merlin and Nimue have had visions of Bedwyr and Guinevere's growing love. When Merlin tells him, Arthur admits that he has known, but he loves and trusts them both and will not interfere with their friendship.

Merlin's relationship with Nimue becomes a matter of love. He has realized for some time that his powers have lessened; Nimue, by contrast, is gaining in power. But aside from a minor regret for certain losses, Merlin is anxious to teach Nimue everything he can, for she will become the "king's enchanter." They go together on several voyages so that he can share his experiences with her. What no one else knows, however, is that Merlin has had several bouts of a falling sickness, presumably a form of epilepsy, which, as a result of the poisoning, have left him unconscious at times, on one occasion for two days. He has one of these spells in the night as he and Nimue visit Ector's castle. Merlin is believed dead and is carried back to Bryn Myrddin (the Crystal Cave), where he is interred.

He awakens a few hours later to find himself shut in, an avalanche of stones, it seems, before the entrance. For the next month he manages to survive; he finds an opening at the top of another part of the cave, but until his former servant Stilicho comes to the area, he has no luck in getting himself out. Other stealthy visitors have come and gone in panic when they heard music from the cave: Merlin's harp has been interred with him.

Merlin spends one month with Stilicho and Mai, the miller's daughter Stilicho has married, recovering his health; not wanting to be seen until he can contact Arthur (who is out of the country momentarily), he goes north by boat, intending to visit Blaise, a former teacher and friend who is living in seclusion and writing a history of the times. At Segontium, however, Merlin comes upon Morgause and her young sons traveling south by boat, seemingly to the Caerleon area and, Merlin deduces, bringing mischief to Arthur. While at Segontium, Merlin goes to the area of Macsen's Tower, where he had long ago found Arthur's sword. A spear and a grail are still among the hidden relics, but he discovers from a shepherd boy that two days before a woman has had these treasures removed.

Merlin immediately travels south again, intent on getting to Arthur. On the way, he intercepts a messenger, who then brings the news to Arthur by means of tokens that Merlin is still alive. Arthur is overjoyed and sets out immediately to meet Merlin. He has just dealt with

Morgause and her sons; the sons would stay with him, Mordred among them, and Morgause would be confined to a nunnery. While Merlin waits for Arthur to come to the appointed place, he finds himself at the mercy of three bandits. Death seems certain until he is rescued by Arthur.

Later, at Caerleon, Nimue comes to visit Merlin, and he realizes then that she is not to blame for the way events turned out. It is she who dug up the spear and grail, having been asked by Arthur to keep them safe for future need and worthy seekers.

Nimue is to marry a prince, a childhood friend, but she will be the leader of the devotees at the chapel on the island in the lake, and Merlin goes back to make his home at the cave at Bryn Myrrdin. He is content there now, looked after by nearby servants (at Arthur's insistence) and visited often by Arthur.

Structure

The novel is divided into four books, each named after a place where Merlin becomes involved in one of the major events. Book I, "Dunpeldyr," is the site of Lot's castle and the scene of the infant massacre. Book II, "Camelot" (Caer Camel), is the fortress town that Merlin helps build and the home then of Arthur, but the main events of this section are Merlin's encounter with Morgause, the effects of the poisoning, and his seven months of wandering. Book III, "Applegarth," is named after the house Merlin builds near Camelot, a place where he is happy with his garden and his studies. This section's main event is the abduction of Queen Guinevere and its aftermath; five subsections are devoted to this incident. Book IV, "Bryn Myrddin," is the name of the cave and the hill that becomes Merlin's final home. The major events here are the premature entombment, Merlin's trials while trying to stay alive and gain his freedom, and the eventual reunion with Arthur.

Everything Merlin has done has been for the sake of Arthur and the kingdom, but it is Merlin's story, and the reader travels with him on these adventures so that actually one sees little of Arthur, except in his conversations with Merlin. Likewise, one sees little of either the first Guenever or the second Guinevere, or for that matter Arthur and Guinevere together. Merlin does not attend the weddings; therefore no details are provided. Guinevere's nature is a mystery to the reader, which makes it easy to assume, as Merlin does in his vision, that Guinevere has sought the company of Melwas and is, despite the golden exterior, a careless and loose woman, though heartbroken at not being able to give Arthur a son.

Characterization

Merlin.   Merlin's vulnerability is especially noticeable in this last novel of the trilogy. He has felt all along that his powers have been leaving him. He still sees visions in the firelight of the bright reflective lights but knows that Morgause would never have been able to drug him in the old days, for his instincts would have warned him and indeed she would never have made the attempt. Merlin's health is undermined by this experience and the effects of being exposed to the elements for seven months, resulting later in the attacks of the "falling sickness."

As Mary Stewart points out, the story of Merlin's madness comes originally from the twelfth-century poem *Vita Merlini,* which is attributed to Geoffrey of Monmouth and is in part a retelling of an older Celtic tale.

Although Merlin becomes most vulnerable in his love for Nimue, he wants to teach her everything he can. In general, he is willing to give over his power, but he does have regrets. Probably the happiest time in his life is the period at Applegarth, his new home, with Nimue at his side. He loves her deeply and she seems to share this love. He wonders later, when he is trapped in the cave, if he misjudged Nimue and if she knew he was not dead but allowed him to be interred; moreover, during his attempts to free himself, he wonders why in her visions she did not see his predicament.

Merlin misjudges Guinevere, in thinking her guilty of a rendezvous with Melwas. He then sees the signs of her fear and realizes she was trying to placate her captor and pretend friendship to stall for time.

Near the end of the novel, as Merlin is being attacked by the three horsemen, he sees in the sky an omen, the black raven, the bird of death. He has been expecting Arthur but now fears that Arthur, coming upon them unawares, may himself be killed in an unequal fight. Merlin is prepared, therefore, quickly to die himself so that they will leave and so that Arthur, if he comes across Merlin's murdered body, will pursue them but at least be fully warned and bring help with him. For the reader, the suspense, as well as the irony, of this unexpected misfortune is great. One has been anticipating the joy of Arthur's reunion with Merlin, and now Merlin is to die before Arthur comes; however, Arthur does come and vanquishes all three criminals.

Among the most suspenseful and painful periods is the time in the cave when Merlin wakes up and realizes he has been left for dead. One experiences his efforts to cope with the darkness and the dwindling supplies; he has been left the ritual cakes and wine, but he does have some dried foods from previous stays. He can tell from the candles that he has been here twelve to fourteen hours. By the simplest of magic, as he calls it, he lights a candle that has apparently blown out. The challenge now is to stay alive. By the use of common sense and the systematic management of objects and supplies, Merlin assesses his situation; here he reminds one especially of Robinson Crusoe as he takes stock of his material goods and invents ways to provide for his needs. Merlin has no tools or books, but he has plenty of candles and there is water. He narrates:

Water, of course, I had; soon after I had come to take up residence in the cave I had had my servant lead a pipe of water from the spring outside to fill a tank; this, kept covered, ensured clean water even through frost and storm. The overflow, channelled to run down to a fissured corner of a remote inner chamber, served as a privy. There were candles aplenty to store, and tinder with the flints on the ledge where I had always kept them. There was a sizable pile of charcoal, but I hesitated, for fear of smoke or fumes, to light the brazier. Besides, I might need the warmth in the time ahead. If my reckoning of time was right, in a short month the summer would be over, and autumn setting in with its chill winds and its killing damp. (419)

He treats setbacks as challenges, but eventually, when he cannot climb the wall of the inner cave that contains the fissure leading to the outside, he becomes depressed. When he cannot contact the solitary wanderers who come by the cave, he begins to despair. On one occasion a grave robber stealthily lowers himself into the cave with a rope, and Merlin, defenseless, decides he must use scare tactics; he therefore pretends to be dead, placing himself on the pall, pulling the king's mantle over himself and putting the gold coins again on his eyes (the gold coins are the ferryman's fee for the journey to the otherworld). Merlin finds this moment of pretense one of the hardest things he has ever done. He thinks, "if I have ever served you, God my god, let me smell the sweet air once more before I die" (438).

Merlin can tell the man is afraid, but when the robber picks up the gold coins, Merlin opens his eyes and says calmly, "Welcome to the hall of the dead, soldier" (440). The man yells out in fear, drops his lantern and the coins, and stumbles back to the hanging rope. After he has gone, Merlin investigates, hoping that the rope was left behind, but that is not the case. God, he feels, has answered him, however. Eventually, when Stilicho comes, a month has gone by, and Merlin's fear is so great that he is in a state of panic until Stilicho helps him to climb out.

Despite the Christian God's increasing influence over the land, Merlin, one finds at last, has not preferred him over the Celtic god. He says, "I had long known that this god brooded no companions. He was not mine, nor (I suspected) would he ever be Arthur's, but throughout the sweet three corners of Britain he was moving, emptying the ancient shrines, and changing the face of worship. I had seen with awe, and with grief, how his fires had swept away the signs of an older kind of holiness; but he had marked the Perilous Chapel—and perhaps the sword as his own, beyond denying" (17–18).

Malory's and Geoffrey's Accounts of Merlin.   In Malory's *Morte d'Arthur* (1485), Merlin is indeed an enchanter. He can change his own appearance, becoming a fourteen-year-old boy or an old man when he chooses, and he can and does transform King Uther into the likeness of Duke Gorlois when Uther secretly visits Ygraine at Tintagel so that she believes he is her husband. Merlin is instrumental in helping Arthur establish his kingship but is dropped from Malory's story after his living burial early in the narrative (Book IV, chapter 1).

In Geoffrey of Monmouth's *The History of the Kings of Britain* (1136), Merlin is dropped from the account immediately after he transforms Uther into Gorlois's likeness. When they marry, Uther and "Ygerna" have two children, Arthur and Anna, both of whom remain at home with their parents. In other words, Arthur is not spirited away by Merlin but grows up in his own household. Neither is Merlin's entombment included in Geoffrey's version.

Nimue.   Nimue is a mysterious character, much more sympathetic than the sorceress of popular legend. She has loved Merlin, but because much else was happening at the time, she has had conflicting visions. Her errands for Arthur have taken her to other parts of the land; she admits to Merlin that at one point the vision came to her of Merlin alive in the cave, but she also saw his rescue and so did not come back from the North. In the meantime she becomes enamored of the prince she is to marry. Merlin has forgiven her, realizing that their relationship could not last. Although Merlin speaks of himself as being aged with impaired health and perhaps looking older than his years, he is actually by novel's end only in his late forties. Mary Stewart has made Nimue a good character in contrast with some of the legendary witchlike characters, reasoning that unless Nimue were of noble sensitivities with good intentions toward Merlin, Arthur would not have allowed her to be his adviser and "enchanter."

Malory's Nimue is burdened with Merlin's excessive attentions: He will not leave her alone. In addition, she believes Merlin is a devil's son, and then when he shows her a cave in a rock that could be sealed, she tricks him into it, casts a spell on him so that he can never come out again, and leaves him there. The knight Sir Bagdemagus comes by and hears him lamenting but cannot move the stone; Merlin tells him that all is in vain, for "he might never be holpen but by her that put him there,"[2] and the knight leaves. In Malory's version, Merlin is entombed shortly after Arthur becomes king; this Merlin has suddenly begun behaving foolishly—all in the name of love—and suffers a degrading end but all according to prophecy.

Mary Stewart explains that the betrayal theme springs originally from the need to explain the disappearance (or death) of a powerful enchanter. Stewart's version of the story is based on a tradition claiming that Merlin, with approaching old age, wanted to pass on his powers to someone who could be Arthur's adviser after his death, thereby depicting Merlin not as a foolish old man but as someone with dignity and sense.

Arthur and Guinevere.   Naturally, Arthur is the focus of much of the attention in *The Last Enchantment* but mainly because Merlin's thoughts are often with him. Young as he is, Arthur has the impossible task of being a leader of men, a man of action, and a good soldier but also a human being, wise, tolerant, and understanding. He loves Merlin and depends on him until Merlin becomes ill. Then the roles reverse, and Arthur seeks to protect and look after Merlin. At this time, though Arthur welcomes Merlin's visions, he has the confidence he needs to be the powerful king who subdues the Saxons and makes allies of the stealthy, sly cronies of King Lot.

Actually, according to Malory, Arthur, not Lot, is the one who orders that all the children born around May Day be put into a ship and set adrift; when the ship is destroyed, all the children die except

Mordred. He, the legend goes, is found by a good man who takes him into his household and then brings him to the king when Mordred is fourteen.

Guinevere, like Nimue, is a shadowy figure. Stewart uses this uncertainty about her character to build suspense, to lead the reader to the wrong conclusions until Merlin is convinced she is innocent in the abduction by Melwas. Then, because Merlin says so, the reader accepts Merlin's judgment as truth.

Stewart says that she was influenced in the creation of her Guinevere by Chaucer's portrait of Criseyde (*Troilus and Criseyde*). Criseyde is honest but weak, if one calls "weak" the helplessness of a woman besieged by men intent on possessing her, men who are using unfair methods (lying and cheating) to pursue their goals. She must at the same time survive and keep herself and her family from being destroyed in honor and reputation. Criseyde, as much as she can be, is honest and sincere in her dealings in a precarious world in which she has little control over her destiny.

In the episode with Melwas, Guinevere is frightened. As the captive she must use her wits to forestall his attack. And, one discovers later, he has threatened that if she tells Arthur the truth, he will say that he has lain with her so that Arthur will kill her as well as Melwas. Guinevere also fears Merlin, for she does not really know him or whether he would poison Arthur against her. Arthur, however, believes Guinevere and is angry when Merlin seems to be suggesting that she may have lied to him. Merlin points out that if Guinevere were afraid, who could blame her for lying to save herself, since Arthur might not have even listened to her but instead killed them both.

Arthur is relieved when Merlin tells him of his vision and reminds Merlin that he does not know much about women. Arthur says, "Does it never occur to you that they lead lives of dependence so complete as to breed uncertainty and fear? That their lives are like those of slaves or of animals that are used by creatures stronger than themselves, and sometimes cruel? Why, even royal ladies are bought and sold, and are bred to lead their lives far from their homes and their people, as the property of men unknown to them" (339). One can see here Mary Stewart's sympathy for the plight of women through the ages and Arthur's sensitivity to Guinevere's harrowing experience.

Arthur says further that sometimes it seems as if Guinevere is "afraid of life itself, and of living." Although she does not fear Arthur, she was afraid of Melwas, and her account of that ordeal coincided with the details of Merlin's vision. Merlin admires Arthur for his compassion and judgment, for his ability to be king and statesman before being the vengeful husband. Arthur loves his wife, and her "barrenness" can in no way persuade him to put her aside. The reader must also admire these traits of loyalty and understanding in Arthur. In fact, his later handling of Bedwyr and Guinevere's supposed love shows his trust and respect for them both. In this novel, however, little is said and almost nothing shown of this affair.

The kidnapping incident has occurred originally in Chretien de Troyes's medieval romance *Lancelot,* in which King Meleagant carries off the queen to his almost-unapproachable kingdom; Malory adopts this event as well. In these accounts Lancelot rescues her; Mary Stewart reminds us that in the various legends Guinevere is abducted from time to time and always rescued by Lancelot.

Even in the early days when Merlin was residing at the Perilous Chapel and Arthur and Bedwyr were coming to visit him, Merlin had seen ominous signs of the shadow of a white owl (the gwenhwyvar) drifting between the two boys. Merlin is reminded of this again in a brief vision as the Welshman from Gwynedd speaks so eloquently of Princess Guinevere as a prospective bride for Arthur, but he says nothing of that to Arthur and instead suddenly finds himself giving warning of an imminent Saxon assault at Badon, to which Arthur and his men go immediately. The Battle of Badon turns out to be the last of the battles for a generation.

Guinevere appears first in the second section of Book III, and she is, as Merlin describes her, a beauty: "hair like golden corn, eyes like summer sky, a flower-fair skin and a lissom body—but add to all this the dazzle of personality, a sort of outgoing gaiety, and a way of communicating joy" (301). She is fascinating to all, but Merlin, on that night when she is brought to Camelot, does notice that Bedwyr is the only one who does not gaze at her constantly, nor does she glance at him; Merlin wonders whether something has happened on the journey on which Melwas and Bedwyr were among her escorts, but nothing further is said about him until much later in the book.

In other versions of the story, Merlin does warn Arthur about Guinevere but in these accounts Arthur has met her earlier and decided he wants to marry her. Further, one sees little of Bedwyr in Stewart's novel; he is the loyal, meditative, quietly heroic, poetic one, the parallel of Lancelot in the tales of Chretien de Troyes and Malory.

The Evil Ones: Morgan and Morgause. The evil characters are Arthur's sisters Morgan (named Morgian in the previous novel) and Morgause. Both are eager to harm Arthur; both become increasingly witchlike, practitioners of potions and spells, their natures power-driven and sexually permissive.

Morgan persuades her lover, Accolon, to steal Arthur's sword Caliburn and then substitute another. Accolon then challenges Arthur to a duel but is killed in the process; however, King Urbgen, unaware of his wife's treachery, remains Arthur's friend. When Morgause, heartless in the incident of the massacred children and guilty of poisoning Merlin, is summoned to the king with her four sons, she finds herself powerless. Arthur will raise the sons, including Mordred, but she will be a virtual prisoner at the nunnery at Amesbury.

A Bit of History

Mary Stewart includes an interesting quasi-historical aspect in the minor characters of Blaise and Gildas. According to Malory, Blaise recorded Arthur's battles, yet no such records have been found. In the novel, Gildas (son of Caw and brother of Heuil) goes to study with Blaise. All these characters are historical. Heuil and Arthur supposedly hated each other. The Welshman Caradoc of Llancarfan wrote that Arthur put Heuil to death, for Heuil was rebellious and lawless; Gildas thereafter became Arthur's enemy. Historically, Gildas became a monk and wrote an account of this age, and though he mentioned the battles in which Arthur fought, he did not mention Arthur. One theory for this omission is that his hatred of Arthur and his disapproval of Arthur's lack of support for the church provoked him into excluding Arthur from his history. In Stewart's novels, though Arthur is baptized a Christian and brought up in Count Ector's Christian household, he is influenced most of all by Merlin, who is like a father to him; he therefore leans more toward Merlin's Celtic gods.

In their discussion of recent Arthurian literature, Taylor and Brewer note that the Merlin figure is becoming increasingly popular. They point out that "the current interest in psychic phenomena and in the powers of the mind makes Merlin a more intriguing figure for the late 20th Century than most other Arthurian characters."[3]

Chapter Eight

The Arthurian Novels: Mordred and Arthur

The Wicked Day

The story idea for *The Wicked Day* (1983), Mary Stewart says, came from the fragments of two sources, Geoffrey of Monmouth's *History* and Malory's *Morte d'Arthur*. This is the tale of Mordred and Arthur, told in the third person omniscient but seen mostly through Mordred's eyes. Stewart did not intend Mordred to be a hero, she claims; nevertheless, he emerges as an entirely sympathetic character with good reason for behaving as he does. After careful research, Mary Stewart found no evidence for the negative Mordred image, since apparently the versions of an evil Mordred were as much an invention as the character of Lancelot, created by the French Arthurian romanticists, was. Until Stewart studied the fragments of the Mordred story in detail, she had assumed he was the villain responsible for Arthur's downfall.

In both *The Hollow Hills* and *The Last Enchantment* Stewart had Merlin foreseeing doom and warning against Mordred's influence. In *The Wicked Day* she tried, she says, to remedy the absurdities found in the traditional legend. Mordred becomes, therefore, a much more believable character, especially since we know that Arthur trusts him and intends (until the end) to make him his heir and that he leaves the kingdom and his queen in Mordred's care when he is in Brittany. If one values the character of Arthur at all, one must trust his judgment, even though by the end of the novel disastrous events and lack of communication have led to the final, fatal conflict.

The Plot

The story begins when Mordred is two years old, living with his foster parents, Sula and Brude, poor natives of the Orkney Islands who are being paid by Queen Morgause to take care of him. They know only that he is a king's bastard, King Lot's, presumably, although Sula, the wife, suspects that he may be King Arthur's son. Because of Morgause's lies, they have been made to fear Merlin and Arthur, believing that Mordred's life is in danger from them; however, it is now again rumored that Merlin is dead.

When Mordred is ten, he rescues Gawain from a precipitous cliff where he has sprained his foot while hunting small eagles. As a result, Mordred is invited by Morgause into her household of four sons: Gawain, the oldest; the twins, Gaheris and Agravain; and Gareth, the youngest. It is time, she has decided, for Mordred to live with them as a son, although she tells him that he is Lot's bastard by an undisclosed mother. Part of her reason, too, is that she sees the boy as a bargaining tool with Arthur; in addition, Mordred has by prophecy been spoken of as Arthur's bane, the eventual cause of Arthur's death. Immediately, however, Morgause orders her young lover, Gabran, to carry out the murder of Mordred's foster parents, Sula and Brude, to ensure their silence.

Four years pass. For Mordred as an outsider, it is sometimes an uneasy existence. Then a summons comes from King Arthur for Morgause and her sons to appear before him. On the way to Camelot they visit Queen Morgan, now a virtual prisoner in her own home because of former misdeeds. Mordred overhears a conversation between the two sisters and believes his life is in danger if he goes to Camelot. He finds now and later, when he hopes to escape, that Arthur's men, supposedly their escort, are guarding him more closely than any of the other members of the party.

Morgause fears Arthur and has brought with her specially crafted items of gold and silver as gifts. It is when Morgause and her family are at the gates of Camelot and Arthur comes out to meet them that he receives word from a hard-riding messenger that Merlin is still alive and leaves immediately to meet Merlin. The boys are taken into the care of Cei to live with the king in Camelot, while Morgause is sent to a convent at Amesbury. Mordred no longer feels threatened.

A few months later, while the household is in Caerleon for the holiday festivities, Mordred discovers in a dice game that Gabran has an amulet that Mordred has made and given his foster mother, Sula, and realizes now who was responsible for Sula's and Brude's deaths. In the confrontation, he kills Gabran. Mordred is sure now that he will be sentenced to death when he is called before King Arthur. Without intending to, Mordred pours out his life story and his anguish to Arthur. At the end of this session, Arthur reveals to Mordred that Morgause is his mother and that he, Arthur, is his father. Mordred is astounded. No public announcement is made, but Mordred is to be treated like a son.

Time passes as the Orkney boys take part in military training; they, too, receive preferential treatment as the king's nephews. Morgause, in the meantime, seeks means to gain her freedom. She influences her sons so that they are not as loyal to Arthur as they might be. Mordred, however, loves his father and has always distrusted Morgause; nevertheless, she has told him of the prophecy. Morgause, who has had several secret lovers, has now chosen one of Arthur's companions, Lamorak. She has circulated word that she is seriously ill and wants to see Arthur. For Arthur's sake, Mordred one evening goes to see if Morgause is telling the truth. He meets her son Gaheris at the convent. As they investigate, they find her drugged waiting women and Morgause in bed with her lover. Gaheris is furious and, in a jealous rage, kills his mother. Mordred helps Lamorak to escape, but Lamorak knows he must leave court now; Gaheris, too, must go into exile and flees to the Northumberland area. Eventually Gaheris and Agravain waylay Lamorak and kill him. This whole series of incidents has lasting and serious effects on the peace and stability of Arthur's court.

Because of increasing troubles on the Continent, Arthur, with a hundred of his men, meets with the Saxon king Cerdic to discuss plans for defending their lands. A group of young Celts are becoming increasingly dissatisfied with present peaceful negotiations. Later on, when King Arthur is on business on the Continent, the young Celts, together with Agravain and Gaheris, break into the queen's quarters and attack Bedwyr, who has been summoned by the queen regarding a letter from the king. In defending himself, Bedwyr kills Agravain and, by mistake, Gareth, the "good" brother; Mordred, trying to keep Gaheris from attacking Queen Guinevere, is also wounded. Later Gaheris, expecting punishment and in haste to get out of Camelot, seeks the ill and delirious Mordred, persuading him that they must flee for their lives, since Mordred too is considered guilty and will be arrested for treason. Once they are safely out of the city, Gaheris leaves Mordred on the doorstep of an isolated monastery in the countryside and rides northward.

In a few days, when Mordred is a bit recovered, he leaves the sanctuary. He has no money and therefore sells his horse and takes a boat north to the islands. Gawain, in the meantime, has become king of the Orkney area. Several months pass during which Mordred assumes the life of a native islander and fisherman, cohabiting with a young widow who has three children in addition to one older child, Mordred's son from the days before he left the islands.

One day as Gawain is riding out on a hunting trip, he meets Mordred working in a field with his son. Mordred then learns that he is not in disgrace, that the queen has told Arthur that Mordred saved her life, and that they know that Gaheris, who is now dead, used Mordred to get out of the city. King Arthur has sought Mordred for months but with no luck. Mordred then goes back to Camelot, where Arthur and Guinevere are relieved and happy to see him.

Events on the Continent in the meantime are turbulent. Arthur takes Mordred with him to Brittany to confer with King Hoel. At Arthur's request and after a frantic letter from Guinevere, who fears the power of the treacherous Duke Constantine, Mordred returns to Britain to take charge while Arthur is gone.

An embassy that Arthur sends to the Roman Quintilianus Hiberus ends in fighting when Gawain in anger attacks and kills Quintilianus's nephew. Arthur, Bedwyr (who has now settled permanently in his family home at Benoic), King Hoel, and Gawain go eastward where there is more fighting. At Arthur's urgent request, Mordred raises and trains troops to send to Brittany. In the wave of fighting that follows, several of the British are wounded and a message comes to Camelot that Arthur has disappeared and is presumed dead.

In Camelot the council hurriedly elects Mordred regent; because of threats of invasion from the Continent, Mordred meets with Cerdic, the Saxon king, and it is determined that they will band together for defense.

Duke Constantine, the son of Cador of Cornwall, has during the years been considered heir to Arthur and the person nominally in charge on the home front. He has been completely uncooperative with Mordred, however, and in fact now writes to Hoel and Bedwyr in Brittany that Mordred is acting in treasonous fashion and intending to consort with Queen Guinevere, neither of which is true.

Storms have kept ships from sailing to Britain, and Bedwyr has been seriously ill. Arthur, back with his forces now, sails to England as quickly as he can, but still no one in Britain has received word that he is alive. Mordred has developed a faithful following of kings and troops. Invasions are expected. A storm drives Arthur's ship to the West Saxon shore. The Saxons fight Arthur and his men as they appear (since the latter are not aware of the treaty made by Cerdic), seeing the

British as invaders. Gawain is fatally wounded in the landing.

Mordred hears of the fighting and comes also, with Cerdic's forces. The Saxons do not know why they are being attacked. Arthur then sees Mordred with Cerdic and assumes Mordred is indeed trying to take over the kingdom for himself. When Mordred sees that the men are Arthur's, he orders his own forces back to Camelot; however, the mis-understandings have caused a permanent rift and suspicion on the part of Arthur. Guinevere has received a letter from Arthur, whom she had thought dead, but now that a battle seems imminent, she leaves in fear for the convent at Amesbury.

Arthur's and Mordred's troops are drawn up opposite each other, and on this last day Arthur and Mordred meet together in parley. Hours pass, the men become restless, the sun beats down; then the thunder of an approaching storm can be heard. When a peaceful settlement seems to have been made, the raising of a silver wine goblet, reflecting the sun, and the sudden drawing of a sword by an officer to kill a snake are misinterpreted as the signals for battle, and the two sides begin the fight.

At the end of the day, Arthur and Mordred meet. Although Mordred does not raise his sword against Arthur, Arthur gives Mordred a fatal wound; Mordred, as he is falling, then strikes at Arthur and in turn delivers a fatal injury. As Mordred lies dying, he hears the voices of Bedwyr and of the weeping women as they carry Arthur off the field to have his wounds dressed. No one attends to Mordred.

Structure

The Wicked Day is composed of a prologue, three books, and an epilogue. The prologue introduces Sula and Brude and their concern for the two-year-old Mordred. Morgause also appears in this section, in her underground chamber probing visions and suddenly realizing that the rumors are not true: Merlin is still alive.

Book I, the longest, is entitled "The Boy from the Sea"; it begins when Mordred is ten and ends with Mordred's discovery of his parent-age. Mordred is the boy from the sea, of course, although many boys in the islands are named Mordred, or Medraut, meaning "boy from the sea." Mordred has escaped the fate meant for him by King Lot when the other newborn infants were set adrift on the sea and died.

Book II is appropriately named "The Witch's Sons." Morgause and her sons have in one way or another caused the breakup of Arthur's circle of companions. The boys are hot tempered, rowdy, and rebellious; it is they, rather than Mordred, who are unreliable and disloyal. The most violent acts in this section are the grisly murder of Morgause by her son Gaheris and the attack on Guinevere and Bedwyr, ending with Mordred's flight back to the Orkney Islands.

Book III, entitled "The Wicked Day," begins with Mordred's return to Camelot from Brittany and, through misunderstandings and misfortunes, leads steadily to the novel's climax—the death of both Arthur and Mordred. One disaster after another causes the rift and the suspicions, but events are plausible under the circumstances. Arthur has become vulnerable and exhausted through extensive fighting; the near death of his best friend, Bedwyr; and the knowledge that they cannot much longer hold the lands of Brittany and must also fight off invasions of Britain. There are also the poisonous message of Constantine, calling Mordred a traitor who intends to take Guinevere as a consort, and Gawain's urging, as he is dying on the Saxon shore, to kill Mordred.

Part of the overall problem is that Justinian, now emperor of Rome and the East, is anxious to regain the lands to the west. Tributes are being demanded of the small kingdoms. Quintilianus Hiberus, with his troops, is Justinian's representative in the West. It is to Quintilianus that the peace embassy is sent, which Gawain immediately turns into a disaster. King Arthur knows, however, that the fighting will come sooner or later with the Roman push to drive out or conquer the Franks and the Celts on the Continent and that eventually Britain too will be threatened.

Most of the novel is seen through Mordred's eyes. Yet there are many times, especially in Book III ("The Wicked Day"), when it is essential to know what is happening simultaneously with Arthur on the Continent and Mordred in Britain. Only through these revelations can the reader see how the misunderstandings develop over time, how these events logically occur, and, near the end, how coincidences, lack of communication, and wrong decisions cause events to escalate and evolve into the final disaster.

In the short epilogue Mordred lies on the battlefield, hearing now the voices calling "The King! The King!"[1] He hears Bedwyr's voice and what must be Nimue's, speaking of seeing to Arthur's wounds. The others, it would seem, are the Ladies of the Lake. They are so close that Mordred can hear the rustle of their gowns and smell their scent.

The voices then fade as the wounded king is carried away. No one has come to seek Mordred.

Characterization

Mordred.   Mordred is very like Merlin in that he is always the outsider. From his childhood on, he must learn to be self-reliant and resilient. Like Merlin for many years, he does not have a father; nor does he know who his mother is. Morgause has told him lies, and he quickly learns that he cannot trust her. He has been told that both Arthur and Merlin wish him dead; he is like Arthur in that even while young he was determined to be somebody. As Nimue says, both had "ambition and desire" (296). Mordred never meets Merlin, but he and Arthur come to love each other as son and father. Mordred at the end of the novel is much like Merlin at the end of *The Crystal Cave*: rejected and alone.

Mordred's four half-brothers, the Orkney sons, are never true friends. They accept him only as a lesser relative, resenting him when Mordred's loyalties are with Arthur rather than Morgause. Later they are jealous of him, but Arthur asks Mordred to be a part of the rebellious group, the young Celts, so that he can know what is happening and forestall serious problems. Because of this involvement, Mordred is present at the attack on Guinevere and Bedwyr. Mordred deplores the behavior of his brothers; only Gareth, the youngest, has his sympathies.

As the underdog, Mordred has always had to struggle for each advantage gained. At one point, when Morgause and the boys are visiting at Morgan's castle while on their way to see King Arthur, Mordred, feeling like a trapped animal, finds a wildcat in a cage and frees it, allowing it to escape through a window; he feels like that wildcat, for at the time he is being guarded by Arthur's men, and he wants desperately to escape and be free from what he fears will be certain death when Morgause and her sons arrive in Camelot.

But even when Mordred is a child he has ambition and a desire to be part of the world on the horizon, the mainland of Britain. His dreams seem always beyond reach, and in the end of the epilogue this wish comes full circle as he lies dying: "Away on the horizon he could see the golden edge of the kingdom where, since he was a small child, he had always longed to go" (305). Later in life, the one person, aside from Arthur, who has been kind to him and shown him affection is Guinevere. From this relationship Mordred has developed a love he tries to hide, and Guinevere is never aware that his kindness to her is anything but that of a good friend. He has assured her that she will always be protected.

Mordred becomes a capable leader of men, respected by them, yet knows that once he has experienced the power of being regent he can never fully go back to being a subject again. Part of the parley process on the last day—one learns from bits of overheard conversation by others—is that Mordred is to have his own lands to govern within the larger kingdom. One never knows otherwise what Arthur and Mordred have discussed in that last talk. The reader at this point sees only what is happening around the two leaders; one gets back to Mordred's thoughts only in the epilogue, when he lies dying, and never discovers what Arthur's thoughts have been during that last day.

Although he is spoken of, Merlin does not appear in this novel. On the afternoon before the final battle, Nimue has begged to see Arthur, telling him that Mordred is not a traitor and would do nothing to harm him; in fact, twice Mordred has sought help in trying to prevent the prophecy. Nimue again comes to Arthur in a dream, letting him know that she and Merlin are interchangeable and reminding him of their talk. Later in Arthur's dream, however, Gawain's ghost appears and tells Arthur to wait for Bedwyr's forces and then attack and kill Mordred, reassuring Arthur that "nothing is treachery if it destroys a traitor" (300). Arthur wakes to find himself speaking these words, indicating perhaps that this is also his own inclination and choice of action.

Stewart borrows the truce incident from Malory's *Morte d'Arthur* (the incident does not appear in Geoffrey's *History*). The truce, however, heightens the uncertainty and drama of the conflict between Mordred and Arthur, and Stewart brings to the event her own creative theories. In her version, Arthur's actions are less obvious and more ambiguous. (In Malory's version, Arthur's intentions to destroy Mordred are clear; he declares the truce only to gain time for the reinforcement of Launcelot's (Malory's spelling) troops from Brittany.)

At the end there is more sympathy for Mordred than for Arthur. Arthur appears fallible and lacking in judgment in this vital moment, for he is receiving and acting on advice from unreliable sources, appearing vulnerable as well where Guinevere is concerned, although there is no more mention of her. Until the last campaign he has continued to be the wise and confident ruler that he has always been. Now he seems weary and confused.

Malory's and Geoffrey's Versions of Mordred. Not much is said about Mordred in either Malory's *Morte d'Arthur* or Geoffrey's *The History of the Kings of Britain,* but in both, Mordred is a negative figure. In Malory, Mordred does not appear in any of the major adventures. One hears of him near the end when, in conjunction with Agravain, they wait for an opportunity to reveal the adultery between Launcelot and Guenever (Malory's spelling), but Agravain appears to be the leader and Mordred the follower. Agravain tells Arthur of their plans and arranges for the king to be temporarily absent (Stewart's Arthur would not have tolerated their accusations). They then launch the surprise attack; Agravain is killed, along with thirteen knights, but Mordred, though wounded, escapes and reports to Arthur.

According to Malory, when Arthur and Gawain are in Brittany waging war against Launcelot, mainly at Gawain's insistence because Launcelot has unwittingly killed all three of Gawain's brothers at one time or another, Mordred is in charge of the kingdom; however, he forges letters to make it appear that the king has been killed in battle and is himself therefore chosen king by the parliament. Mary Stewart uses this incident, but in her story a declaration of the king's being missing in battle has actually come and no further word arrives until it is too late. In Malory, Mordred tries to marry Guenever but she escapes him and hides in the Tower of London. Strangely enough, once Arthur arrives in Britain, many of the people side with Mordred and favor him more than Arthur.

In Geoffrey's version there are no surprise raid on the Queen and no mention of the queen's activities. Here, Mordred takes over the kingship and lives with Guinevere, the news of which prompts Arthur's return from his on-to-Rome campaign.

Arthur. King Arthur's first appearance in *The Wicked Day* is climactic, for there has been a progressive building of events toward this meeting. The preparations have continued for months, even before the summons from Arthur comes, with Morgause preparing the treasures that she would present at their meeting. Then, for Mordred there has been tremendous anxiety, since he believes that Arthur is his enemy and that he will be put to death.

Stewart's Arthur is a man of power and stature. He has tremendous control and confidence, seen in the way he deals with Morgause; he also feels much anger toward Morgause, whom he holds responsible for

Merlin's supposed death. To gain a sympathetic audience, Morgause has appeared with her family before she was expected, hoping thereby to be received in the main hall before Arthur's companions, but when she and her family are announced Arthur comes out alone in the night. This action is highly unusual and totally unexpected by all. There are apprehension and even, on Morgause's part, fear, although in trying to hide her emotions she appears imperiously in control. Mordred is fascinated by all he sees:

Mordred could never afterwards say what made the first sight of the High King so impressive. No ceremony, no attendants, none of the trappings of majesty and power; the man was not even armed. He stood alone, cold, silent, and formidable. The boy stared. Here was a solitary man, dressed in a brown robe trimmed with marten, dwarfed by the range of lighted buildings behind him, by the trees that lined the roadway, by the spears of the armed guards. But in fact, in all that ringing, frosty, dusk-lit space, none of the party had eyes for anything but that one man. (112)

Suspense increases with the long silence, since Arthur's plans for Morgause's party are unknown. Stewart manages this scene expertly, in a deliberately measured pace. After Morgause's initial plea for clemency, there is no reply from the king—only silence, no movement of welcome. Mordred senses the awesomeness of the moment, and though he is looking down, he feels something as strong as a touch and finds Arthur's "eyes fixed on him . . . charged with a look that sent a thrill through him, not of fear, but as if something struck him below the heart and left him gasping" (113). His fear is gone.

Mordred understands, then, that this king would not stoop to vengeance on the lowly bastard (as he supposes himself) of King Lot, a dead enemy, and realizes that Morgause's threats have been lies. At this critical moment he determines to do whatever is needed to win a place and favor with this king. Arthur finally raises Morgause to her feet and asks the children to wait at the gatehouse while he speaks to their mother. One does not know what is said, but shortly afterward the courier arrives with urgent news. After consulting with the messenger, the king suddenly swings around and shouts. He gives what appear to be battle orders, and his huge gray war stallion is brought. Servants come running with his sword, and as the gates swing open, Arthur rides out "with the speed of a thrown spear" (115).

When Cei comes to get the boys, they discover (as does the reader unfamiliar with an earlier version of this scene in *The Last Enchantment*) that Merlin, Arthur's greatest friend, previously thought dead, has been seen, and a joyous Arthur rushes off to meet him. Arthur demonstrates here the anger he feels toward Morgause, then directly after, the love and loyalty of which he is capable, as he hurries to be with the long-lost Merlin.

Other memorable scenes in which Arthur displays important elements of his character include his meeting with Mordred after Mordred has killed Gabran. Arthur shows compassion and vulnerability when he hears Mordred's story and then confesses to him that he is Mordred's father and that Morgause is his mother. Arthur shows deadly but controlled anger when well-meaning people, including Mordred, suggest that Guinevere and Bedwyr are more than friends. He is completely supportive of both the queen and Bedwyr and has great sympathy for the queen's loneliness and childlessness. His preoccupation is with ruling the kingdom, and he is often absent from home. He is at the same time the peaceful, highly competent commander of his forces when he meets to sign a treaty with the Saxon leader Cerdic.

Arthur also has a sense of humor and loves his dogs and horses, but he becomes more and more serious as the novel progresses, frustrated and weary with the misdeeds of those around him, his nephews especially. He is forgiving, perhaps to a fault, and he does make mistakes. One is told that he judges wrongly regarding Gawain when he considers him suitable for the mission to Quintilianus; in fact, the omniscient speaker says, "Arthur as seemed his fate whenever he had to deal with Morgause's brood and blood, was mistaken" (253). The young Celts, of whom Gawain is one, blamed Arthur at home for his adherence to Roman forms of law and centralized government, yet in Brittany Arthur is prepared to resist Roman attempts to regain control of the Celtic territories. Mordred can see the irony of the situation. Arthur, too, is a fighter, showing personal courage in insisting on one-to-one combat with the giantlike man, head of the ruffian band that has raped and murdered King Hoel's niece in Brittany and has for some time terrorized the inhabitants of the countryside.

Arthur sends Mordred back to Britain after receiving Guinevere's frantic message about the ominous nature of Duke Constantine's movements and intentions. Even though the reader may know what is going to happen, there is suspense in seeing how events will cause this turnabout in trust on Arthur's part. The foreshadowing comes as the omniscient speaker resumes the narration about Arthur and Mordred's parting in Brittany: "So, in mutual trust, they talked, while the night wore away, and the future seemed set as fair behind the clouded present as the dawn that slowly gilded the sea's edge beyond the windows. If Morgause's ghost had drifted across the chamber in the hazy light and whispered to them of the doom foretold so many years ago, they would have laughed, and watched for the phantasm to blow away on their laughter. But it was the last time that they would ever meet, except as enemies" (254).

Perhaps it is in the dream sequence on the night before the final battle that reader sympathy definitely shifts from Arthur to Mordred. A boy in the guise of Nimue but with Merlin's eyes is suggesting to Arthur what Nimue had said the day before: that Arthur, Nimue, and even Merlin have let themselves be blinded by the fateful prophecy. Nimue says that "fate is made by men, not gods." She continues to urge Arthur to reconsider his actions. Mordred does not wish to harm Arthur. She says:

Our own follies, not the gods, foredoom us. The gods are spirits; they work by men's hands, and there are men who are brave enough to stand up and say: "*I am a man; I will not.*" [Mordred has done this] . . . If he [Mordred] could seek to defy the gods, then so, Arthur, can you. Lay by your sword, and listen to him. Take no other counsel, but talk with him, listen, and learn. Yes, learn. For you grow old, Arthur-Emrys, and the time will come, is coming, has come, when you and your son may hold Britain safe between your clasped hands, like a jewel cradled in wool. But loose your clasp, and you drop her, to shatter, perhaps for ever. (299)

But Arthur is not inclined to listen; the parleying might have come to a stalemate had not decisive action come, at the end of the hours of deliberation, from the troops by mistake. Yet even this action could have been halted had Arthur really wanted it so.

Stewart's Arthur is a more human, likeable person than his counterpart in the works of either Malory or Geoffrey of Monmouth. In Malory's *Morte d'Arthur,* Arthur, after the first few books, is kept in the background. Early in the narration (Book V of twenty-one), he has achieved tremendous military successes and is crowned emperor of Rome by the pope. Arthur then leaves those lands to return to Britain, and from there the adventures of the knights are foremost. Arthur does order the death of the infants when it is prophesied that a baby born on May Day will destroy him. He does intend faithfully to follow the law of the land when Guenever is thrice condemned to be burned at the stake. He also admits, on the last occasion, that he is more upset over losing his good knights than his queen, since one can always get a queen. Further, he bemoans the leaving of the goodly number of knights in the pursuit of the Holy Grail, for he fears that this distraction will cause the breakup of the Round Table. In the end, it is Arthur's war on Launcelot (urged on by Gawain) that causes his extended absence from Britain and the end of his reign.

The Arthur of Geoffrey, in contrast, is a fierce fighter, a man wholly absorbed by the constant warfare necessary to establish his empire. In this process, which takes years, he subdues a number of kingdoms, including Scotland, Ireland, Gaul, Iceland, Denmark, and Norway, and has a reputation, one is told, that spreads to the ends of the earth. He is on his way to attack Rome when word arrives that Mordred has established himself as king and is living with Guinevere.

Bedwyr and Guinevere.   Bedwyr's character has not changed from that in the previous novels. He remains the stalwart, quiet, honorable friend of both Arthur and Guinevere. He fights fiercely to protect the queen from attack, and though a deep attachment is evident between them, there is no indication of an affair. Earlier Nimue (in *The Last Enchantment*) has seen a vision of their love, but there is no evidence that they acted upon these feelings. They take pains to behave honorably.

When Bedwyr kills Gareth and Agravain, he knows he must leave Britain. He has attacked Mordred, too, not realizing that Mordred was trying to protect Guinevere. After Bedwyr leaves for his boyhood home in Brittany, he marries and in so doing removes himself as a rival for Guinevere's affections. Bedwyr's near death affects Arthur deeply, but Bedwyr does recover, coming to Arthur's aid in the final battle and being at hand during Arthur's last moments. As mentioned previously, many modern novelists have reverted to the earlier versions of the Arthurian legends, as does Mary Stewart, choosing Bedwyr (Bedivere) instead of Launcelot as Guinevere's lover.

Guinevere's behavior is consistent with that in *The Last Enchantment*. She would willingly accept Mordred's friendship and protection when she believes Arthur dead. She has come to rely on Mordred and his daily briefings about events as they affect the kingdom. She has never before been treated as an equal. Mordred has the fantasy of marrying Guinevere, and one has the feeling she might have considered the possibility. She fears most of all being a cast-off queen. Mordred feels he has had a glimpse of "the real Guinevere, a lonely woman afraid of life, a leaf to be blown into a safe corner by any strong wind. He would be—was—her safety" (280).

When Guinevere receives the letter from Arthur just before the battle—her first evidence that he is alive—she is told that Arthur and Mordred are at war. Her terrified reaction is that she is lost; whether she fears that Arthur may consider her too much in Mordred's favor one does not know. Her behavior is ambiguous, but she leaves immediately for the convent at Amesbury.

The person she has feared most is Constantine, and she had reason to distrust him; he is not the noble person that his father was, being instead ambitious and treacherous, anxious to destroy Mordred. And although one never meets him, except by hearsay, one is conscious that he is a man of power. Ironically, according to Geoffrey, Constantine becomes king when Arthur and Mordred die, and he kills Mordred's two sons: The one son the reader has met is in the Orkney Islands, and the other by Mordred's mistress, is in northern Britain. While Mordred was living at Camelot, he also had a house in town that Arthur encouraged as a place where the restless young Celts might meet yet be under supervision. Mordred's mistress lived here until Mordred left for the Orkney Islands, but one knows nothing about her.

Malory's "Guenever". The "Guenever" of Malory differs in personality and character from Stewart's queen. Though she is beautiful and generous, she is also more independent, bold, and even shameless in her relationship with Launcelot. Theirs is almost an open affair, and they consistently tempt discovery. When she is kidnapped by Meliagaunt (see Melwas in *The Last Enchantment*), she is not conciliatory and fearful, as is Stewart's queen, but berates him for his behavior and the dishonor he brings to himself and the king as a knight of the Round Table. "Traitor Knight," she says, "Thou shamest all knighthood and thyself, and me I let thee wit [know] shalt never shame, for I had lever cut mine own throat in twain rather than thou shouldst dishonour me."[2]

In Malory also this Guenever tricks Mordred at the end, when he has gained unlawful control of the kingship, and escapes to the Tower of London, fortifying herself there rather than marry him. She answers his messages by saying that "she had lever slay herself than to be married with him."[3] But this Guenever has also been brought to the stake ready to be burned three times until each time rescued by Launcelot. The first time the knights of the court believe she is responsible for poisoning one of their group, Sir Patrise, at a feast given by her (she is innocent), but no knight will defend her. Many say, "As for our most noble King Arthur, we love him and honour him . . . , but as for Queen Guenever we love her not, because she is a destroyer of good knights."[4] In the other two trials at the stake, she is accused of adultery (rightfully).

Moreover, Malory's Guenever is often jealous where Launcelot is concerned and unjust in her treatment of him. Once, as a result of her anger, he runs off mad (crazy) into the woods and remains there for two years until regaining his sanity. At the end of the story, it is Guenever and Launcelot's affair and Arthur's war on Launcelot in Brittany that then destroy the knighthood and, eventually, Mordred and Arthur. Guenever becomes a nun and Launcelot then also joins a religious order, dying purposely, not long after Guenever.

In Geoffrey's *The History of the Kings of Britain,* Guinevere receives little mention, since the major part of the account deals with Arthur's battles against his foreign enemies. In one short paragraph, between accounts of battles, one is introduced to Arthur's bride: "Finally, when he [Arthur] had restored the whole country to its earlier dignity, he himself married a woman called Guinevere. She was descended from a noble Roman family and had been brought up in the household of Duke Cador. She was the most beautiful woman in the entire island."[5]

Later, after Arthur has defeated Iceland, as well as Norway, Denmark, and Gaul, she is mentioned with Arthur as receiving their guests in celebration at a great feast. The next time she is spoken of is when Arthur, about to march on Rome, receives word that Mordred has "placed the crown upon his own head. What is more, this treacherous tyrant was living adulterously and out of wedlock with Queen Guinevere, who had broken the vows of her earlier marriage."[6] She apparently considered this a suitable arrangement, and Mordred was not as unattractive as one might have been led to believe. The last mention of Guinevere comes after Arthur has landed in Britain and begun warfare with Mordred, when the queen, giving way to despair, flees to take vows in the church of Julius the Martyr, "promising to lead a chaste life."[7]

In Stewart's version, of course, there are two women in Arthur's life: Guenever—who is brought up in the household of the Duke of Cador, was originally Ygraine's lady-in-waiting, and dies of a miscarriage within the first year of her marriage to Arthur—and Guinevere. This Guinevere might have married Mordred had the conditions been right and had she been convinced Arthur was dead. In Stewart's tale, emphasis is not on the marriage or love relationship between Guinevere and Arthur or Guinevere and Bedwyr. The focus is on Merlin and Arthur in the first three books and on Mordred and Arthur in the last. In the latter book, of course, Morgause and her four sons also play a major part.

The Orkney Witch.   As in the previous novels, Morgause continues to be the major evil character, although she has a much larger role in this novel. Her hatred for Arthur motivates most of her actions. She is still attractive and able to manipulate others as she sees fit but at the same time becomes more dangerous, more dissolute, and more reckless. At the convent she has a comfortable life, surrounded by her belongings, but, of course, it is freedom she wants. At one point when Mordred visits her and she has been expecting Arthur (although he does not come), she and her ladies have removed the costly rugs, the wall hangings, and other expensive furnishings, leaving only a few pieces of furniture in a bare room and thereby giving the appearance of living in pitiful circumstances. Mordred sees the evidence of this trickery.

The scene of Morgause's death is presented in grisly detail. But she is not gone, for her influence lives on in her sons, who seek revenge on her lover, and thereafter one act of violence begets another. Bit by bit the camaraderie of Arthur's court is destroyed, and when the destructive elements on the Continent appear, the present way of life and the peaceful reign are ended.

Sula and Brude.   As in the previous novels, the poor people are often the most noble in *The Wicked Day*. Such is the case with Mordred's foster parents, Sula and Brude, living in the Orkney Islands. Brude is a fisherman. Stewart says of him, "Though rough-seeming and slow-witted, he was an honest man and good at his trade" (12). His wife, Sula, is four years younger than he, only thirty-three, but she is bent by rheumatism and already looks like an old woman. She loves Mordred and fears above all else the day when he will be taken from her. As it happens, Gabran, Morgause's young lover, brings the contaminated wine as a present from Morgause when the ten-year-old Mordred has been invited to live in her household, and when the two are drugged and insensible, Gabran burns down their house. Mordred is deeply shocked by this tragedy and does not suspect until many years later that it was a planned execution.

As seen previously, Stewart's poorer classes are usually hardworking, sincere, and, as with Sula and Brude, unselfish and giving of love. Her attention to detail is evident in the way she depicts her characters' environment, the result of careful research. For instance, here, after describing the surrounding countryside, she focuses on Sula and Brude's small house:

> The cottage walls were built of stones gathered from the storm beach. These were flat slabs of sandstone, broken from the cliffs by wind and sea. . . . No mortar was used, but the cracks were caulked with mud. Each storm that came washed some of the mud away, and then more had to be added, so that from a distance the cottage looked like nothing more than a crude box of smoothed mud, with a thatch of rough heather-stems capping it. The thatch was held down by old, patched fishing nets, the ends of which were weighted with stones. There were no windows. The doorway was low and squat, so that a man had to bend double to enter. It was covered only with a curtain of deerskin, roughly tanned and as stiff as wood. The smoke from the fire within came seeping in sullen wisps round the edges of the skin. (12–13)

Stewart describes also their simple clothing, but with Sula and Brude, one learns, there are incongruities in their possessions, since some objects have been purchased by money paid them to care for Mordred. Obviously the sum was not much, but they have blankets, tolerable food, and a sturdy fishing boat beached outside the house, objects they might not otherwise have had.

Most often in these novels, description is integrated with the story line. One is seldom conscious of extraneous details; only rarely, as in the illustration above, does Stewart give a more intricate explanation and this for the purpose of reader understanding of the primitive life-style of these early Orkney inhabitants.

Addenda

Less is said about religion or the Christian God in this novel; one good reason is that the deities of the Orkney Islands are the Celtic gods, as they are also of Morgause and of all the major characters. The role of prophecy is like that in the Greek world; the prophecy of Mordred's being the bane of Arthur is like that of Oedipus who is to destroy his father, and Mordred, like Oedipus, is guilty also of desiring to marry his father's wife, who is not his real mother but his step-mother. Actually, Guinevere may have been closer in age to Mordred.

Arthur was a young father, perhaps only fourteen when Mordred was born. Despite what Nimue says about man standing up to the gods and being able to change his destiny, nothing in this novel disproves the prophecy. What has been prophesied does happen. While one can forestall or hurry up the result or change its character, the event occurs nevertheless.

Here and at the end of the other novels, Mary Stewart has provided an "Author's Note" in which she discloses her sources and the reasons for telling her tale as she did. She points out here that Camlann is the site of Arthur's last battle and that scholars place the date of the battle somewhere between A.D. 515 and 539. She suggests, however, that a date somewhere about 522–527 "seems reasonable," but the actual location of the battle is uncertain. Stewart says she has chosen the regions of South Cadbury in Wiltshire, maintaining that the "hill at South Cadbury has, owing to recent excavations, a strong claim to being an Arthurian strong point, possibly Camelot itself. Hence there seemed no need to look further for the site of the final battle."[8]

As indicated earlier, Mary Stewart drew elements of *The Wicked Day* from both Geoffrey of Monmouth and Sir Thomas Malory. The title of the novel came from Malory's account of the events of that last day. Sir Lucan tries to persuade Arthur, after a long day of fighting and after everyone else on his side has been killed (except Sir Bedevere and Sir Lucan), to forget about Mordred, whom Arthur now seeks. Mordred is then seen leaning wearily upon his sword "among a great heap of dead men."[9] Arthur calls for his spear, and Sir Lucan says, "Sir, let him be. . . . for he is unhappy; and if ye pass this unhappy day ye shall be right well revenged upon him. . . . God of his great goodness hath preserved you hitherto. . . . Ye have won the field, for here, we be three alive, and with Sir Mordred is none alive; and if ye leave off now this wicked day of destiny is past." But Arthur will not listen and runs toward Mordred, crying, "Traitor, now is thy death day come."[10] Mordred, in turn, runs toward Arthur, who thrusts his spear into Mordred's body, and as Mordred falls forward, he strikes Arthur with his sword, inflicting the mortal blow.

In Geoffrey's version, Mordred dies during the day's fighting but not by Arthur's hand, and Arthur receives his mortal wound from someone else and is carried off the battlefield.

A major difference between Malory's and Geoffrey's tales of Arthur is that in Geoffrey, Arthur remains the focus of attention, as he is the center of the action in almost all the medieval English accounts. Malory, who takes as his source the later French romances, shifts the focus from Arthur to the knights of the Round Table fairly early in his story. The invented character of Launcelot becomes the major focus of the French versions and of Malory's account; Tristram and Gawain also receive much attention. In the course of the narration, Malory repeatedly uses the phrase "as the French book sayeth," reminding the reader of the source of his story; nevertheless, there are also significant differences between Malory and the writers of the French romances, mainly in his downplaying of the Grail quest and his giving to the love interest a subordinate position.

Chapter Nine

Conclusion

The Suspense Novels

Obviously there are major differences between Stewart's suspense novels and her Arthurian tales. Her main purpose in the earlier works is to tell an exciting story, and one finds in them definite patterns in her handling of the characters and working out of the action. The two suspense novels that vary significantly from the pattern are *The Ivy Tree* and *Touch Not the Cat,* both set in England and among the most effective stories. In these, the narrative patterns are intricate, since in *The Ivy Tree* the story line deals with an impersonation and tricks the reader into accepting the reliability of the main character and in *Touch Not the Cat* the narrative pattern is complicated by the impressionism created by the character's telepathic powers and the interweaving of the story of a second (at first, nameless) narrator. The heroines here are struggling with the problems of their lives, but in the process there is also a high level of suspense. Both novels are fine examples of sophisticated storytelling techniques.

The heroines of the other nine suspense novels share similar qualities; in fact, they merge as almost one character starring in a series of episodes, and their names are elusive. Yet the similarity is not important, since the emphasis is not so much on characterization as on plot, nor does it detract from the liveliness and individuality of the stories. The typical protagonist is English, between twenty-two and twenty-eight years old, off on vacation in an exciting part of the world, attractive, bright, willing to be her brother's keeper and to become involved in the rescue of someone younger or less fortunate than she. She does not seek conflict but because of her adventurous and compassionate nature finds herself in the middle of it. Since she is honest and trusting, she does not always recognize the villain, but neither does anyone else, and sometimes puts her trust in the wrong person. The villain of Stewart's stories is not easily recognizable, for he is often charming, handsome, and, on the surface, reliable. Because the tales are narrated in the first person, the reader experiences the same shock as the heroine does when she discovers, alas too late, that here is a villain. Since the stories also involve murder—past, present, or attempted—mistakes of this kind can be serious. At the same time, the heroine may distrust the good man who seems to be evil, because he is often a mysterious, shadowy figure with questionable motives, all of which are clearly understood and found worthy by the end of the story.

Mary Stewart uses the chase as a major technique for suspense, and the protagonists are an important part of the chase, not as weak, brainless individuals (although fear is normally present), not as helpless victims, but as independent, more nearly equal, intelligent human beings. In the different novels the chase itself varies in nature and duration. In most cases, the heroine literally runs from the villain in a matter of life or death—at least she perceives it as such—but sometimes the chase is by automobile, as it is in Stewart's first novel, *Madam, Will You Talk?*

When the chase is on foot, it is often complicated by bad weather conditions or a treacherous terrain, as it is in the fog and mountains of the Isle of Skye in *Wildfire at Midnight* or the stormy night and treacherous mountain waters of the Pyrenees in *Thunder on the Right*. Sometimes the chase is extended over a longer period, as occurs in *Nine Coaches Waiting* with Linda Martin and nine-year-old Philippe running and hiding for twenty-four hours before they are finally safe. Another extended chase takes place in *The Moon-Spinners,* in which the two young men are being hunted by the Turkish villain as Nicola Ferris, aiding them, finds herself in danger and before the chase ends almost loses her life.

One of the most complicated chase patterns occurs in *Airs above the Ground* as Vanessa March runs from Sandor Balog and then with Lewis and Timothy follows Sandor to his contacts; later in the process of running for help she must chase and stop the morning train before it reaches the helpless Timothy, caught on the cogwheel railroad track. Chases in *My Brother Michael* and *This Rough Magic* end in physical fights in which the heroine is involved. Physical violence is present in most of the stories, and in eight of them the villains die violent deaths.

The chase as Mary Stewart uses it requires space and therefore takes place in the open countryside, in the mountains, or on a body of water. And except for the short interval in Marseilles in *Madam, Will You Talk?* the chase is never within a city or town. Perhaps one of the main reasons that the chase technique has appealed to Stewart is that she is comfortable in the out-of-doors, and so are her characters. She knows about the trees and the flowers, the birds and the rocks; she also has a painter's eye and a poet's ear and as a result creates passages of excellent description. Thus, for her, it would seem, the chase is a natural choice in building a good story.

Most of the suspense plots involve crime and murder. The crime in five of the novels has to do with smuggling, usually drugs; in one case, with counterfeit money. One novel deals with jewel thieves, another with stolen arms and gold. Three of the novels have land and inheritance claims as the source of the trouble. The most unusual motive for murder is found in *Wildfire at Midnight,* in which the psychotic killer has immersed himself in the culture of the Celtic gods and is making sacrifices to them.

In Mary Stewart's world the good people are pitted against the bad, but identifying the villains is not made easy, since tricking the reader is part of the suspense technique. The good people must fight to restore order and good. This assumption is the underlying theme of Stewart's suspense novels and, in a sense, of her Arthurian tales as well.

The characters are not contemplative or excessively intellectual, nor do they spend time with philosophical debates or even melancholy reminiscences. They are doers, people of action, not bystanders. All in all, the women protagonists are charming but strong, assertive, and often instrumental in solving the mystery or crime and in helping to remedy a bad situation. As Anthony Boucher has stated in *The New York Times Book Review,* "Surely there are few more attractive young women in today's popular fiction. Intelligent, humorous, self-reliant yet highly feminine, these girls are as far removed as you can imagine from the Idiot Heroine who disfigures [at least for men] so much romantic fiction."[1]

Thornyhold (1988) belongs to the family of suspense stories but does not follow the same patterns. Gentler and less suspenseful, it begins with the lonely childhood of Geillis Ramsey (Jilly) in northern England and follows her into adulthood when Geillis inherits the home of a favorite though mysterious lady relative, who is fey and witchlike, an herbalist and healer. Later, living at Thornyhold, Geillis has as her nearest neighbor a young country woman who also has witchlike tendencies, concocting potions and medicines but without the talent apparently to achieve the desired results. Conflict arises over the attentions of a widowed writer living nearby and whom Geillis wins. Although the book is beautifully written and has a quiet charm, it has not received the critical or popular acclaim of Stewart's previous novels.

The Arthurian Novels

Stewart's Arthurian novels are, in contrast to her suspense novels, much more serious. The historical novel must be as accurate a picture of the times as is possible, and the earlier the age, the more difficult the task. The fact that in this case there are many legends forces the writer to choose sources carefully, and the earlier sources (Geoffrey of Monmouth and so on) are becoming more popular as present-day novelists are bypassing the more famous, romanticized versions of Chretien de Troyes, Malory, and Tennyson.

Mary Stewart wanted to create a Merlin who was a child and then follow him through his life. Most Merlins in King Arthur stories are not only old men but often bizarre and ridiculous.

Whereas the suspense novels take place within a short period (two or three weeks) and in one specific location and seldom include more than a dozen characters, the Arthurian tales are epic. Their story lines become complicated, for the time spans cover many years (approximately sixteen years in *The Crystal Cave*); they involve many locations in Britain and Brittany and, as in *The Hollow Hills,* other countries as well, and they include many characters. Indeed, characterization becomes much more important in the Arthurian tales. The people become more real, more memorable. One sees them in many different situations. Character development now becomes necessary, and while the plot flows along without the pace or urgency of the suspense novel, there is always a building of a series of situations and complications. Furthermore, the ending of these novels is not necessarily happy, nor have the good people always triumphed, but the sympathy is with them nevertheless. Mary Stewart's Arthurian stories do not include the search for the Holy Grail, nor do they include the adventures of the knights (companions) as such or make much mention of the Round Table, stories created (after Geoffrey of Monmouth) by the French romance writers.

Raymond H. Thompson in *Return from Avalon* has said that "modern fiction tends to humanize traditional figures. One result of this is that characters are less often completely good or bad than in romance."[2] This "humanizing" treatment is true of Stewart's characters as well.

The major characters—Merlin, Mordred, Arthur, Guinevere, Bedwyr, and Nimue—are all essentially good people, if sometimes flawed. They behave as honorably as they can under the circumstances and have concern for what is best for Britain, but as with normal people, their lives become complicated not only through their own weaknesses but, more often, by people who interfere in their lives and by events over which they have little control. Mordred is swept along by the misadventures of his half-brothers, although he tries to remain neutral. Similarly, Arthur becomes victim of the passions of Morgause and her sons and of the ill luck and confusing elements of the times. Guinevere is not the strong queen that Ygraine was, but neither does one see evidence of Guinevere's infidelity, whereas Ygraine was willing to take King Uther as her lover (in *The Crystal Cave*) as long as she thought her husband, Duke Gorlois, would not be harmed by the affair. Neither Ygraine nor Uther, of course, could foresee Gorlois's death, nor were they directly responsible.

As with the suspense novels, these works are skillfully written in a compelling and poetic (though not obviously so) prose style. Mary Stewart understands both her characters and her readers. She has an instinctive sense of drama and the elements that create tension and suspense.

Stewart's novels are also alike in that they contain strong women characters. In the suspense novels all the protagonists fit this designation; in the Arthurian tales although there are fewer women characters most of them are staunch survivors, solid people from both the upper and lower classes. Among them, after Ygraine, are Merlin's mother, who will not be pressured into marriage or reveal the name of Merlin's father, and Merlin's nurse, Moravik, who watches over him when he is young and then takes charge of the young Arthur in Brittany. Also in this category are Ygraine's waiting woman Marcia and the young nursemaid Branwen (in *The Hollow Hills*), who travels with the infant Arthur and the rest of the party through the dangers of the Perilous Forest to the temporary one in Brittany; Nimue, the new enchantress, Merlin's assistant and beloved companion, becomes an authority figure as she gains in power. Also strong and able to exert power, but evil, are Morgan and Morgause, Arthur's sisters.

Guinevere is a notable exception, for she is a good woman, although not a secure one. She is, however, more scrupulous and moral than her counterparts in either Malory's *Morte d'Arthur* or Geoffrey's *The History of the Kings of Britain* and certainly more sympathetic.

As in the suspense novels, although there is no emphasis on the ugly, Mary Stewart does not shy away from realistic details, and perhaps the incident most shocking to the reader is the beheading of Morgause by her son Gaheris. In contrast, however, the reader of Malory is struck by the numerous accounts (although not in great detail) of beheadings and maimings in the adventures of the knights. For example, one notably bizarre event involves Gawain, who is assigned the task of bringing back a white deer that had appeared in the great hall at the wedding feast of Arthur and Guenever. After a long chase, Gawain, with Gaheris, follows the deer into a castle and kills it. The master of the castle is upset, since his wife had given him the deer, and arms himself for the battle with Gawain. Gawain knocks him to the ground and, not giving mercy, intends to kill him. Just at the moment when Gawain is to strike off the man's head, the lady of the castle throws herself on the man's body and Gawain cuts off her head by mistake. A few more incidents follow, but Gawain must then carry the dead woman (along with the deer's head) to Camelot, her body in front of him as he rides and her head tied around his neck.[3] For gory detail, nothing in Mary Stewart's novels, needless to say, quite equals that.

It is generally agreed that no novel of recent times has been as influential in producing popular interest in Arthurian matters as T. H. White's *The Once and Future King* (1958). Although White uses Malory as his primary source, his book contains many differences in comic treatment, character, and situation. His Merlin is an absentminded magician who helps to educate the boy Arthur by transforming him into various animals and states of being. As Jennifer Goodman points out in *The Legend of Arthur in British and American Literature,* "The idea of Merlyn's education of Arthur has continued to fascinate writers as different in character as Thomas Berger and Mary Stewart."[4] Goodman mentions as well the tremendous popular success of Stewart's novels and says that "at least some credit for the wave of popular Arthurian literature in the late 1970s and the early 1980s should be given to Mary Stewart."[5]

Rosemary Sutcliff is another of the many effective historical novelists cited by authorities. In *The Return from Avalon,* Raymond Thompson states that "Sutcliff was the first to give Launcelot's role to Bedwyr, the companion who with Kay is most closely linked to Arthur in earliest tradition, but her lead has been followed by both Bradshaw and Stewart."[6] Gillian Bradshaw's trilogy is classified as fantasy, although her novels present much realistic detail about this Dark Ages world. Her forces of good include Merlin and Arthur, whereas Morgause, Morgan le Fay, (and unlike Stewart's conception) Nimue, and Mordred are among her forces of evil.

One of the most widely read of recent Arthurian novels has been

Marion Zimmer Bradley's *Mists of Avalon* (1982), told from Morgaine's point of view. Bradley uses Malory as a source and her Merlin is the title of the head Druid, but she, like Mary Stewart, features a Guinevere who is vulnerable and insecure.

Mary Stewart's novels, both the suspense stories and the Arthurian tales, continue to be popular. The readers who became fans of the earlier stories were even more enchanted with the later novels. Stewart continues to be praised for her fine prose style, for her skill in creating plot, and for the psychological realism of her characters. Her Merlin, Arthur, and Mordred are memorable.

It is difficult to think of the four Arthurian novels individually since they are all part of a larger pattern, but perhaps the two finest works are the first and the last of the series, *The Crystal Cave* and *The Wicked Day*. Each involves the growing up of the main character amid obstacles and hostility. Part of the mystery and suspense derives from the solution to the identity of these characters, Merlin and Mordred; the characterizations are expertly drawn, and the pacing is consistent. In *The Crystal Cave* the plot leads to the one event at the end of the novel, the conception of Arthur. In *The Wicked Day* the major events lead to the inevitable climax, the deaths of both Mordred and Arthur and the destruction of the court of Arthur.

The plots of these novels are more integrated than those of *The Hollow Hills* and *The Last Enchantment,* for although the plot in *The Hollow Hills* leads up to the crowning of Arthur, the progression of events from Arthur's conception to his kingship is of necessity uneven and the pacing is less consistent. In *The Last Enchantment* the fading of Merlin from a place of importance causes a lessening of suspense and perhaps interest, yet for most readers these supposed objections are not serious flaws and in no way impair the enjoyment of these novels or an appreciation for the sensitive and satisfying portrait of Merlin. All four works are excellent representations of the Arthurian world and among the finest historical (or quasi-historical) novels available today.

Notes and References

Chapter One

1. "About Mary Stewart" (New York: William Morrow & Co., 1970), 4 (pamphlet).
2. Ibid., 5.
3. Ibid., 7.
4. Nan Robertson, "Behind the Best Sellers," *New York Times Book Review,* 2 September 1979, 18.
5. Roy Newquist, "Mary Stewart," *Counterpoint* (New York: Simon & Schuster, 1964), 564.
6. Kay Mussell, "Stewart, Mary," in *Twentieth Century Romance and Gothic Writers,* ed. James Vinson (Detroit: Gale Research, 1982), 646.
7. Ibid., 647.
8. Mussell, "Preface," in *Twentieth Century Romance and Gothic Writers,* ed. James Vinson (Detroit: Gale Research, 1982), vii.
9. Newquist, "Mary Stewart," 564.
10. Deborah A. Straub, *Contemporary Authors,* vol. 1, ed. Ann Evory (Detroit: Gale Research, 1981), 637.
11. "Teller of Tales," *The Writer* 83 (May 1970):12.
12. "Setting and Background in the Novel," *The Writer* 77 (December 1964):7.
13. Ibid., 9.
14. Ibid., 8.

Chapter Two

1. *Madam, Will You Talk?* (1955; reprint, New York: M. S. Mill and William Morrow & Co., 1956), 164; hereafter cited in the text as *MWYT.*
2. *Wildfire at Midnight* (Greenwich, Conn.: Fawcett, 1956), 144; hereafter cited in the text as *WM.*
3. Newquist, "Mary Stewart," 569.
4. *Nine Coaches Waiting* (1958; reprint, New York: M. S. Mill and William Morrow & Co., 1966), 241–242; hereafter cited in the text as *NCW.*

Chapter Three

1. F. W. J. Hemmings, "Mary Queen of Hearts," *New Statesman,* 5 November 1965, 698.
2. *My Brother Michael* (New York: M. S. Mill and William Morrow & Co., 1966), 299–300; hereafter cited in the text as *MBM.*

3. Aristophanes, *The Frogs* (New York: M. S. Mill and William Morrow & Co., 1966), 33. Quoted by Mary Stewart as heading for chapter 3 in *My Brother Michael*.

4. *The Ivy Tree* (1961; reprint, Greenwich, Conn.: Fawcett Crest, 1963), 272.

5. *The Moon-Spinners* (1962; reprint, London: Coronet Books, Hodder and Stoughton Paperbacks, 1986), front cover; hereafter cited in the text as *MS*.

Chapter Four

1. William Shakespeare, *The Tempest,* act 5, scene i.

2. Shakespeare, *The Tempest,* act 5, scene 1. Lines used in beginning of chapter 9 in *This Rough Magic* (New York: M. S. Mill and William Morrow & Co., 1964), 133.

3. *Airs above the Ground* (New York: M. S. Mill and William Morrow & Co., 1965), 255.

4. Artemus Ward (Charles Farrar Browne), "A Visit to Brigham Young." Used as chapter 14 heading in *Airs above the Ground,* 188.

5. *The Gabriel Hounds* (New York: M. S. Mill and William Morrow & Co., 1967), 57.

6. Samuel T. Coleridge, "Christabel." Lines quoted in *The Gabriel Hounds,* 88.

7. *Touch Not the Cat* (New York: William Morrow & Co., 1976), 7; hereafter cited in the text as *TNC*.

Chapter Five

1. Geoffrey Ashe, *The Quest for Arthur's Britain* (1968; reprint, London: Paladin Grafton Books, 1971), viii.

2. Beverly Taylor and Elisabeth Brewer, *The Return of King Arthur: British and American Arthurian Literature Since 1900* (St. Edmunds, Suffolk: St. Edmundsbury Press, 1983; New York: Barnes & Noble, 1983), 303.

3. Ashe, *The Quest for Arthur's Britain,* x.

4. *The Crystal Cave* (New York: William Morrow & Co., 1970), 509–10; hereafter cited in the text.

5. "Author's Note," *The Crystal Cave,* 525.

Chapter Six

1. "Author's Note," *The Hollow Hills* (New York: William Morrow & Co., 1973), 398; hereafter cited in the text.

2. Ashe, *The Quest for Arthur's Britain,* 32.

3. Stewart, "Author's Note," *The Hollow Hills,* 400.

Chapter Seven

1. *The Last Enchantment* (New York: William Morrow & Co., 1979), 13; hereafter cited in the text.
2. Sir Thomas Malory, *Le Morte d'Arthur*, vol. 1 (Middlesex, England: Penguin Books, 1969, 1986), 124.
3. Taylor and Brewer, *The Return of King Arthur*, 313.

Chapter Eight

1. *The Wicked Day* (New York: William Morrow & Co., 1983), 305; hereafter cited in the text.
2. Malory, *Le Morte d'Arthur*, vol. 2, 429.
3. Ibid., 506.
4. Ibid., 382.
5. Geoffrey of Monmouth, *The History of the Kings of Britain* (Middlesex, England: Penguin Books, 1966; 1986), 221.
6. Ibid., 257.
7. Ibid., 259.
8. "Author's Note," *The Wicked Day*, 313.
9. Malory, *Le Morte d'Arthur*, vol. 2, 513.
10. Ibid., 514.

Chapter Nine

1. Anthony Boucher, review of *My Brother Michael*, *New York Times Book Review*, 10 April 1960, 28.
2. Raymond H. Thompson, *The Return from Avalon: A Study of the Arthurian Legend in Modern Fiction* (Westport, Conn.: Greenwood Press, 1985), 176.
3. Malory, *Le Morte d'Arthur*, vol. 1, 98–104.
4. Jennifer R. Goodman, *The Legend of Arthur in British and American Literature* (Boston: Twayne Publishers, 1988), 101.
5. Ibid., 106.
6. Thompson, *The Return from Avalon*, 175–76.

Selected Bibliography

PRIMARY WORKS

Novels

Madam, Will You Talk? London: Hodder & Stoughton, 1955; New York: Mill, 1956.

Wildfire at Midnight. London: Hodder & Stoughton, 1956; New York: Appleton Century Crofts, 1956.

Thunder on the Right. London: Hodder & Stoughton, 1957; New York: Mill, 1958.

Nine Coaches Waiting. London: Hodder & Stoughton, 1958; Yew York: Mill, 1959.

My Brother Michael. London: Hodder & Stoughton, 1960; New York: Mill, 1960.

The Ivy Tree. London: Hodder & Stoughton, 1961; New York: Mill, 1962.

The Moon-Spinners. London: Hodder & Stoughton, 1962; New York: Mill, 1963.

This Rough Magic. London: Hodder & Stoughton, 1964; New York: Mill, 1964.

Airs above the Ground. London: Hodder & Stoughton, 1965; New York: Mill, 1965.

The Gabriel Hounds. London: Hodder & Stoughton, 1967; New York: Mill, 1967.

The Wind off the Small Isles. London: Hodder & Stoughton, 1968.

The Crystal Cave. London: Hodder & Stoughton, 1970; New York: Morrow, 1970.

The Hollow Hills. London: Hodder & Stoughton, 1973; New York: Morrow, 1973.

Touch Not the Cat. London: Hodder & Stoughton, 1976; New York: Morrow, 1976.

The Last Enchantment. London: Hodder & Stoughton, 1979; New York: Morrow, 1979.

The Wicked Day. London: Hodder & Stoughton, 1983; New York: Morrow, 1983.

Thornyhold. London: Hodder & Stoughton, 1988; New York: Morrow, 1988.

Novel Collections

Three Novels of Suspense: Madam, Will You Talk?, Nine Coaches Waiting, and *My Brother Michael.* New York: Mill, 1963.

The Spell of Mary Stewart: This Rough Magic, The Ivy Tree, and *Wildfire at Midnight.* New York: Doubleday, 1968.
Mary Stewart Omnibus: Madam, Will You Talk?, Wildfire at Midnight, and *Nine Coaches Waiting.* London: Hodder & Stoughton, 1969.
Triple Jeopardy: My Brother Michael, The Moon-Spinners, and *This Rough Magic.* London: Hodder & Stoughton, 1978.
Selected Works: *The Crystal Cave, The Hollow Hills, Wildfire at Midnight,* and *Airs above the Ground.* London: Heinemann, 1978.

Juvenile Fiction

The Little Broomstick. Leicester: Brockhampton Press, 1971; New York: Morrow, 1972.
Ludo and the Star Horse. Leicester: Brockhampton Press, 1974; New York: Morrow, 1975.
A Walk in Wolf Wood. London: Hodder and Stoughton, 1980; New York: Morrow, 1980.

Play Collections

Radio Plays: *Lift from a Stranger, Call Me at Ten-thirty, The Crime of Mr. Merry,* and *The Lord of Langdale,* 1958.

Nonfiction

"About Mary Stewart" (pamphlet). New York: William Morrow & Co., 1970.
"Setting and Background in the Novel." *The Writer* 77 (December 1964): 7–9.
"Teller of Tales." *The Writer* 83 (May 1970):9–12, 46.

SECONDARY WORKS

Biography

Commire, Anne, ed. "Mary Stewart." In *Something about the Author,* vol. 12. Detroit: Gale Research, 1977, 217–19. Brief biographical information, including career, writings, and interests.
Mussell, Kay J. "Mary Stewart." In *Twentieth Century Crime and Mystery Writers,* 2d ed., edited by John M. Reilly, 823–24. New York: St. Martin's Press, 1985. Includes brief biographical information but discussion centers on Stewart's novels (see "Critical Studies" section below).
Mussell, Kay J. "Mary Stewart." In *Twentieth Century Romance and Gothic Writers,* edited by James Vinson, 645–47. Detroit: Gale Research, 1982. Concise biographical facts. Discussion focuses on Stewart as writer (see "Critical Studies" section below).

Newquist, Roy. "Mary Stewart." In *Counterpoint.* New York: Simon and
    Schuster, 1964, 562–71. The interview in Edinburgh, the basis for this
    chapter, took place November 1963. Includes elements of biography and
    material about Stewart's own books; ideas about writing, characteriza-
    tion, and plotting; reaction to reviews; and the novelists and playwrights
    she admires.
Robertson, Nan. "Behind the Best Sellers." *New York Times Book Review,* 2
    September 1979, 18. A biographical account, including highlights of
    personal life and of writing habits and how Stewart came to write the
    Merlin trilogy. Says that by 1979 (according to William Morrow & Co.),
    25 to 30 million copies of Stewart's books had been sold in America.
Smaridge, Norah. "Mary Stewart." In *Famous British Women Novelists.* New
    York: Dodd, Mead & Co., 1967, 117–22. Mainly biographical material
    but also includes discussion about specific novels and their backgrounds.
    Notes that the general reader finds Stewart's novels as "spellbinding" as
    Jane Eyre or *Rebecca.*

Critical Studies

Ashe, Geoffrey, ed. *The Quest for Arthur's Britain.* 1968. Reprint. London:
    Grafton Books, 1986, x. Includes essays by Ashe, Alcock, and others.
    Covers background material, legend and fact about Arthur and his
    world. Discusses some of the excavations and discoveries providing new
    information.
Duffy, Martha. "On the Road to Manderley." *Time,* 12 April 1971, 95–96.
    Discusses some of the more popular women's romantic suspense novels;
    says the field is "dominated by Victoria Holt, the most prolific writer,
    and Mary Stewart, the most accomplished." Also gives brief biographies
    of Mary Stewart, Elizabeth Goudge, and Victoria Holt.
Fries, Maureen. "The Rationalization of the Arthurian 'Matter' in T. H.
    White and Mary Stewart." *Philological Quarterly* 56 (1977): 258–65.
    Finds that many modern novelists feel the challenge to "rationalize"
    Arthurian matter. There are disparate treatments, however, as seen in the
    works of Stewart and White: In general, White's treatment is comic,
    Stewart's serious. Both deal with just rule and human frailty.
Goodman, Jennifer R. *The Legend of Arthur in British and American Literature.*
    Boston: Twayne Publishers, 1988, 7, 106. A comprehensive, compact,
    well-organized study of the origins of Arthur and Arthurian literature
    through the ages, ending with a discussion of the literature of the twen-
    tieth century. Mentions Mary Stewart.
Hemmings, F. W. J. "Mary Queen of Hearts." *New Statesman* 70 (5 November
    1965): 698–99. A good article, deploring Stewart's lack of recognition
    and praising the "cleanness of her style" and the "astringency of much of
    her observation." Says that her novels are concocted according to a for-

mula but that there is "nothing machine-made in the devising." Includes several of the novels in discussion. Says her success is well earned.

Herman, Harold J. "The Women in Mary Stewart's Merlin Trilogy." *Interpretations: A Journal of Ideas, Analysis, and Criticism* 15 (spring 1984): 101–14. Notes Stewart's vivid portrayal of women who are often stronger and more clever than the men and dominate them. This concept of women marks a difference between Stewart's trilogy and earlier Arthurian works. Calls Stewart's Igerne (Ygraine) the finest portrayal of this character in the entire body of Arthurian literature and Stewart's Guinevere one of the most sympathetic.

Hoberg, Thomas. "A Whistle for the Wind: Mary Stewart's Merlin." *Avalon to Camelot* 2, (1987): 17–19. An essay that praises Stewart's conception of Merlin, allowing the reader to know the real Merlin, the Merlin who is also used ruthlessly by his god as a means of launching Arthur into the kingship. Says that only Mary Stewart has brought Merlin "to life in such a way that his legendary deeds (and in one way or another, she includes them all) compel us to empathize with the poignantly vulnerable man behind the sorcerer's mask."

Lacy, Norris J., ed. "Mary Stewart." In *The Arthurian Encyclopedia*. New York: Peter Bedrick Books, 1987, 528. Briefly gives plot of the four Arthurian novels; says that Stewart's "characters' psychology is mostly convincing" and that "in her use of Merlin's and Mordred's *enfances,* she restores to twentieth century readers one of the most popular medieval Arthurian modes of explaining subsequent plot and character."

Malory, Sir Thomas. *Le Morte d'Arthur,* vol. 1 and 2. 1969. Reprint. London: Penguin Books, 1986. Accounts of the life and death of Arthur and his knights, based largely on the French romances. Basis for most of the popular Arthurian legends.

"Mary Stewart." In *Contemporary Literary Criticism,* vol. 35, edited by Daniel C. Marowski, 388–97. Detroit: Gale Research, 1985. Very helpful. Includes reviews of most of the novels through *The Wicked Day,* as well as an excerpt from *The Writer* in which Stewart discusses her own work. The introduction credits Stewart with "bringing higher standards to the genre of romantic suspense novels" and mentions that her novels are "well received critically due to her entertaining stories and skillfully crafted prose."

"Mary Stewart." In *Contemporary Literary Criticism,* vol. 7, edited by Phyllis Mendelson and Dedria Bryfonski, 467–68. Detroit: Gale Research, 1977. Not very complete. Consists mainly of an excerpt from Hemmings's article "Mary Queen of Hearts" and single, brief reviews of *My Brother Michael, Airs above the Ground, The Hollow Hills,* and *Touch Not the Cat.*

Monmouth, Geoffrey of. *The History of the Kings of Britain.* 1966. Reprint. Harmondsworth, Middlesex, England: Penguin Classics, 1986. Geoffrey

traces the history (often fictional) of the Britons through nineteen
hundred years, from Brutus through Cadwallader (A.D. 689). Stewart's
major source for her Arthurian novels. Helpful introduction by Lewis
Thorpe, 1976.

Mussell, Kay J. "Mary Stewart." In *Twentieth Century Crime and Mystery Writers*, 2d ed., edited by John M. Reilly, 823–24. New York: St. Martin's
Press, 1985. Gives critical praise for Stewart's excellence in the genre;
calls them "literate" and "intelligently developed" novels, avoiding
cliché; mentions also Stewart's "extraordinary descriptive writing."

———. "Mary Stewart." In *Twentieth Century Romance and Gothic Writers*, edited by James Vinson, 645–47. Detroit: Gale Research, 1982. Says that
Stewart's original and excellent romances "relied heavily upon her ability
to evoke a place, to create complex characters and to weave sophisticated
and compelling stories." Says Stewart's "heroes and heroines are people
of commitment especially to others and to abstract concepts of truth and
justice" but that she "portrays her characters so sensitively that they remain believable."

Starr, Nathan Comfort. *King Arthur Today: The Arthurian Legend in English and
American Literature, 1901–1953*. Gainesville: University of Florida Press,
1954. This is seen as the pioneering work on modern Arthurian studies,
but it treats material only up to 1953. Excellent discussions; however,
much important material (twice that in the volume) has been written
since the 1950s.

Straub, Deborah A. "Mary Stewart." In *Contemporary Authors*, vol. 1, edited
by Ann Evory, 636–38. Detroit: Gale Research, 1981. Some biographical material but mainly a good discussion of Stewart's novels, integrating
various reviews of her works through *The Last Enchantment*.

Taylor, Beverly, and Elisabeth Brewer. *The Return of Arthur: British and American Arthurian Literature*. Bury St. Edmunds, Suffolk: St. Edmundsbury
Press, 1983, 13, 303–6, 314. Begins with and concentrates on the
Arthurian literature of the nineteenth century but brings the study
through 1981. Calls Stewart's *The Crystal Cave* (1970) one of the most
successful Romano-British Arthurian romances. Says that the "characters
are depicted in terms of modern psychology and moral attitudes and set
against a romanticized fifth century Romano-British society" and that in
Stewart's work "Arthur's England is idealized; the brutalities which some
other writers stress do not appear in her books." The differing tone "contributes to the success of these works in both England and America."

Thompson, Raymond H. *Return from Avalon: A Study of the Arthurian Legend
in Modern Fiction*. Westport, Conn.: Greenwood Press, 1985, 17, 50–52,
55–57, 172, 174, 176. Discusses especially the large volume of work
published in the past thirty years; divides the material into realistic fiction, historical fiction, science fiction and science fantasy, and simple
fantasy. Names Stewart as one of those doing careful research, examining

various original texts and works of scholarship, and being a trained scholar herself.

Selected Book Reviews

Madam, Will You Talk?

"Also Noted." *Saturday Review* 39 (17 March 1956): 43. Calls this novel "slickly plotted."

Boucher, Anthony. *New York Times,* 18 March 1956, 43. Says "a backward glance will reveal coincidences and inconsistencies . . . but so unusually skillful that you don't really care."

"Mystery and Crime." *New Yorker* 32 (24 March 1956): 151–52. Calls this a "neatly contrived" chase and Mary Stewart's first effort "very promising."

"The New Mysteries." *Time* 67 (19 March 1956): 116. Says this is a "fast chase in polished prose . . . an outstandingly sleek example of the feminine first-person ('Had I but known . . . ')." Mentions the "colorfully painted backdrops of provincial France and the Marseilles waterfront."

Wildfire at Midnight

Boucher, Anthony. *New York Times Book Review,* 9 September 1956, 35. Says this is a "suspense story of low probability but high romantic freshness and readability. In weighing faults and virtues, virtues win out." Says that "setting . . . [is] depicted with vivid wonder," that here is another of Stewart's "captivatingly spirited heroines," and that "the story is rich in uncertainty, excitement and sheer narrative flow."

Sandoe, James. *New York Herald Tribune Book Review,* 9 September 1956, 8. Calls this novel frail but diverting.

Thunder on the Right

Schiller, Barbara. "A Highly Charged Thriller." *New York Herald Tribune Book Review,* 5 October 1958, 6. Says that as in Stewart's previous books the author "once again proves herself adept at writing a highly charged romantic mystery thriller distinguished for the excellence of its setting, the charm of its heroine and the breathtaking urgency of action."

Nine Coaches Waiting

"Books." *New Yorker* 34 (17 January 1959): 94. Calls this "feminine novel of romance and suspense expertly written."

Boucher, Anthony. "Criminals at Large." *New York Times Book Review,* 18 January 1959, 20. Says the novel, though perhaps designed for feminine readers, can be enjoyed by male readers as well. Says that of current practioners of the suspense novel he "can't think of anyone aside from du Maurier, who tells such stories as well as Mary Stewart." Calls *Nine Coaches Waiting* "the longest and probably the best to date."

Ross, Mary. "Cinderella Arrives at Chateau Valmy." *New York Herald Tribune,*
8 March 1959, 8. Some of the "dark passions of Jane Eyre combined with
the 'Cinderella' theme make this a stirring suspense story." Calls this a
novel not easy to put down.

My Brother Michael

Boucher, Anthony. *New York Times Book Review,* 10 April 1960, 28. Says that
if Stewart's "delightfully entertaining" novels have a fault, it is that "their
plots . . . cannot survive a backward glance" but that here in this novel
"even this flaw vanishes."

Pym, Christopher. "It's a Crime." *The Spectator* 204 (18 March 1960): 401.
Calls this so far the best of the novels. Says "slightly sentimental over-
tones, but the Greek landscape and—much more subtle—the Greek
character are splendidly done, in a long, charmingly written, highly
evocative, imperative piece of required reading for an Hellenic cruise."

Ross, Anne. "Fine Place for a Romance." *New York Herald Tribune Book Review,*
14 August 1960, 8. Calls Mary Stewart one of the "leading writers in a
field which blends suspense with romance and drama." Says that the "em-
pathy and respect" between hero and heroine are most satisfying and that
in Stewart's "portrait of Greece past and present she has presented the
most exciting background of all."

The Ivy Tree

Boucher, Anthony. *New York Times Book Review,* 7 January 1962, 36. Says it
is hard to think of anyone more insistently readable than Mary Stewart.
Says she "carries on a delicate and meticulous game of wits with the
reader."

Gitomer, Irene. *Library Journal* 86 (15 December 1961): 4309. Says that this
"involved novel of impersonation and inheritance reads more like Daphne
du Maurier" and that the "author's easy narrative style, her vivid descriptions of Northumberland countryside, the sharp delineation of her stock
characters, her neat, contrived resolution, and her impeccable good taste
guarantee satisfaction to fans of the genre."

The Moon-Spinners

Feld, Rose. "Love and Suspense on Crete." *Books,* 7 April 1963, 14. Says that
"besides weaving a fine story, Miss Stewart can create young people who
are warmly and refreshingly their age."

Marsh, Pamela. "The Landscape of Suspense." *Christian Science Monitor,* 3
January 1963, 13. Says that readers will not be disappointed with this
novel; "they will be tangled in suspense while their imaginations move
in an unfamiliar countryside whose loveliness is made strangely lovelier
by sudden, darkening mystery."

This Rough Magic

Boucher, Anthony. *New York Times,* 16 August 1964, 20. Calls this "a magical concoction brewed from the most disparate plot elements" and "a warm and sunny book, for all its violence; even its crimes (in the proper spirit of 'The Tempest') give delight and hurt not."

Rennert, Maggie. "Teapot Tempest." *The Sunday Herald Tribune,* 15 November 1964, 22. A lukewarm review, even though she says, "The author is an old, sure hand and makes a very smooth magic indeed of exciting goings-on on Corfu."

Airs above the Ground

Boucher, Anthony. *New York Times Book Review,* 24 October 1965, 46. Says this is "one of Stewart's best—which means escape fiction at its most enchanting."

Hughes, Dorothy B. *Sunday Herald Tribune,* 21 November 1965, 35. Says that "Miss Stewart embroiders her invigorating plot with her gifted sense of scene in one of the most effective of her novels."

The Gabriel Hounds

Daltry, Patience M. "More of the Stewart Magic." *Christian Science Monitor,* 28 September 1967, 11. Wonders "what the secret of the Stewart magic is that keeps readers so loyal. Is it predictability?" Says "this all makes excellent escape fiction."

Earle, Adelaide. *Chicago Tribune,* 31 March 1968, 10. Says that this is an "engrossing yarn" and that Stewart's "use of the history of Lady Hester Stanhope is fascinating"; also that Stewart "obviously knows the Eastern countries she is writing about. But the women's matinee aura is unmistakable."

The Crystal Cave

Grady, R. F. (S. J.) *Best Sellers* 30 (15 July 1970): 158. Says that "those who have read and enjoyed the many novels of Mary Stewart . . . will not need to be told this is an expertly fashioned and continually absorbing story, with a facile imagination fleshing out the legend of the parentage of the future King Arthur—and, too, of Merlin himself."

Levin, Martin. *New York Times Book Review,* 9 August 1970, 33. Says that "Miss Stewart (better known to most readers for her top-drawer suspense novels) lightens the Dark Ages with legend, pure invention and a lively sense of history."

Taylor, Nora E. "Mary Stewart Conjures Merlin." *The Christian Science Monitor,* 3 September 1970, 13. Calls this an absorbing, carefully researched story but finds that the "uncertainty of the inclusion of magic lends a certain falseness."

The Hollow Hills

Minudri, Regina. *Library Journal* 98 (15 June 1973): 2016. Says that there is "not the caricature, mystic or eccentric of other Arthurian novels. Merlin is human and readers will understand and sympathize with and like him. Witchcraft and Wizardry are played down, and the story moves swiftly as Arthur advances toward his inevitable glory as High King. Sure-fire exciting reading."

Publishers Weekly, 28 May 1973, 35. Says that this novel is "romantic, refreshing and most pleasant reading" and that Stewart "has steeped herself well in the folklore and known history of fifth-century Britain and makes of her . . . warlords lively and intriguing subjects."

Weir, Sister Emily. *Best Sellers* 33 (15 July 1973): 191–92. Calls this no mere sequel but a strong novel standing on its own right; also says that the author exhibits "the same deft handling of suspense which has made her novels with a more contemporary setting so popular." Praises the characterization, that of Merlin in particular. Says that Stewart gives one a "feeling for the century about which she writes." Recommends the book to readers who appreciate the "spell of well-chosen words and the art of a superior raconteur."

Touch Not the Cat

Foote, Audrey C. "Cat on a Tudor Roof." *Washington Post*, 15 August 1976, E1, E4. Though she says that Ashley Court is a "fictional cliché" and "most of the characters are one-dimensional, and there are other gimmicks," she adds that "none of this matters or it merely adds to the charm. . . . The really solid pleasure is watching a professional architect at work." Says that "this novel is a blueprint on how to handle exposition" and that "the story of Ashley Court is not a very original construction, but it is certainly one of the best made of its kind."

Weir, Emily, C.H.S. *Best Sellers* 36 (November 1976): 250. Says that though the novel lacks the rich background of the author's Arthurian works, "it does have marvelous suspense with all the trappings of a superior gothic novel." Calls the characters "believable persons."

The Last Enchantment

Levin, Martin. *New York Times Book Review*, 2 September 1979, 9. Calls this an "adult fairytale, a perfect trip out of the present into a dark but cozy age in which political problems can be settled by Excalibur and personal problems by witchcraft." A rather superficial, unsatisfying review.

McClellan, Joseph. "In the Days of Swords and Sorcery." *The Washington Post*, 22 July 1979, C6. Says that readers may find this third volume of the trilogy anticlimactic if they have unrealistic expectations, since they will not see much of Arthur; that Merlin is no longer the center of the action; and that there is the problem of Merlin's infatuation with Nimue, "all of

which Stewart handles well." Says that Stewart "does splendidly in bringing alive the Dark Ages of the original Arthur" and that "Arthur and
Merlin stand as forces of reason, peace and order."

Todisco, Paula J. *School Library Journal* 26 (October 1979): 164. Maintains
that this novel does not equal the other two in vitality and drama; speaks
of the difficulty of the receding Merlin and finds the ending a "little
unsatisfying."

The Wicked Day

Hoffman, Roy. *New York Times Book Review,* 1 January 1984, 20. Says that in
almost every way this is a "highly enjoyable romance . . . a provocatively
recast legend." Calls Mordred and Morgause's sons the best characters in
the book. Says that "by the time Mordred and Arthur meet their inevitable fate, many convincing characters have surfaced."

Mills, Mary. *School Library Journal* 30 (March 1984): 178. Says Stewart "has
created flesh and blood characters out of legends"; calls this a "well-plotted, passionate drama," more "historical than mystical."

Stoppel, Ellen Kaye. *Library Journal* 108 (15 September 1983): 1809. Says
that "although this is a familiar story, the reader is caught up, eager to
learn how Stewart handles Merlin's prophesy of doom. Fifth century Britain—its terrain, lifestyle, inhabitants—is vividly described."

Index